QUICK & EASY MEDITERRANEAN DIET FOR BEGINNERS

Tomato and Garlic Bruschetta, *page 42*

Quick & Easy

MEDITERRANEAN
DIET *for* BEGINNERS

100 HEALTHY RECIPES

LINDSEY PINE, RD, MS

**ROCKRIDGE
PRESS**

Interior and Cover Designer: Jane Archer
Art Producer: Meg Baggott
Editor: Adrian Potts
Production Editor: Jax Berman
Production Manager: Martin Worthington

Cover photo ©2021 Darren Muir; Food styling by Yolanda Muir.
Rua Castilho/StockFood USA, ii, 50; Irina Tarzian/Shutterstock, v; Annie Martin, vi; Nadine Greeff/Stocksy, x; Darren Muir, 4; CarinaBöttcher/StockFood USA, 20; Emily Triggs/Stocksy, 36; Cameron Whitman/Stocksy, 64; JuliaHoersch/Gräfe&Unzer Verlag/StockFood USA, 78; Maximilian Carlo Schmidt/StockFood USA, 108; Marta Muñoz-Calero Calderon/Stocksy, 130; Marti Sans/Stocky, 156; SKC/Stocksy, 172.

Illustrations ©2021 DeMih/Creative Market

Cover image: Gnocchi with Broccoli Rabe, Sun-Dried Tomatoes, and Pine Nuts, page 98

Paperback ISBN: 978-1-63807-049-8
eBook ISBN: 978-1-63807-732-9
R0

To my Husband.

Thank you for being my best friend and supporting me through this journey called life.

Contents

Introduction

There is something magical about Mediterranean cuisine. You can feel that the food is about more than sustenance. It's about a lifestyle full of flavor and enjoyment. The first time I traveled to countries along the Mediterranean Sea—including France, Spain, and Italy—I fell in love with the Mediterranean diet, even though I was only 21 and had never even heard of it at the time. Little did I know, this style of eating includes cuisines from many countries around the Mediterranean Sea, including ones in North Africa and the Middle East.

Multiple members of my family have suffered cardiac events, so I focus on recipe development for heart-healthy lifestyles in both my personal and professional life. Many chronic diseases are preventable if you have a healthy lifestyle. In fact, the American Heart Association estimates that up to 80 percent of cardiovascular disease is preventable. That is a truly eye-opening statistic! I consider the Mediterranean diet a deliciously appealing way to move toward greater whole-body wellness. Whether you want to help prevent heart disease and other chronic diseases or need to manage an existing diagnosis, this healthy way of eating works.

Doctors, registered dietitians, and other health professionals recommend the Mediterranean diet because it is one of the most researched eating patterns out there. Yes, I am talking about actual, evidence-based science! In eating this way, you'll get plenty of important health-promoting components such as fiber, protein, heart-healthy fats (including omega-3 fatty acids), antioxidants, phytochemicals, vitamins, minerals, and more. Year after year, news outlets such as the *US News & World Report* rank the Mediterranean diet as the best overall diet. Not only is this eating pattern easy to follow and delicious, but it also works for people with busy lives, hectic schedules, and a variety of health goals.

The great thing about this diet is that it is not a "diet" in the typical restrictive way we think about that dreaded "D" word. The Mediterranean diet is an overall eating pattern that is sustainable for the long term. It consists of a loose set of suggestions that guide your food choices. I love that it emphasizes the foods you should be eating more of instead of telling you that certain foods are off-limits. You can even extend the principles of the Mediterranean dietary pattern to the cuisines of other cultures, such as those of Latin and South America, Japan, or Scandinavia!

I also love how easy it is to work the Mediterranean Diet into "normal" cooking schedules, whether you're cooking for just you or for you and your family. You don't have to spend all day in the kitchen cooking complicated dishes. Because there are so many different flavors and ingredients to work with, you can satisfy family members with many different taste preferences while also adding quick and easy creations to your cooking repertoire. I know that learning to eat in a new way can be daunting, but it doesn't have to be. That's where this book comes in!

This book will help make home cooking easy and enjoyable, with quick and easy dishes that fit into various cooking strategies—one-pot, five-ingredient, time-bound, freezer-ready big batches, and even no cooking required. People have been eating a Mediterranean diet for thousands of years across many countries, so you're not likely to run out of recipe ideas once you learn how varied and enjoyable this way of eating can be.

Here's you can expect to find in this book:

◆ Guidelines and health benefits of the Mediterranean diet

◆ Quick, easy, and delicious recipes that fit into specific, easy strategies

◆ Healthy, whole-food ingredients that are easy to find in your local grocery store

I am confident you will love the Mediterranean diet as much as I do, and I am so excited to share my love of this style of food with you. Healthy eating doesn't have to be difficult or monotonous. Because you have the flavors of so many countries to work with, the possibilities are practically endless. If you're looking to eat healthy and actually enjoy the food, this way of eating is for you. You can do this, so let's get cooking!

Chapter One

A Way of Life

Congratulations on taking the first step to a healthier lifestyle! The actions you take today will help you reap sustainable, long-term benefits. Luckily, the principles of the Mediterranean diet are simple and can fit almost any lifestyle. There aren't any strict rules to follow, and you get to eat real, delicious food. This chapter will show you why this eating pattern is beneficial to your health, how easy it is to follow, and what types of delicious foods and cuisines are involved. Everything you need to start living the Mediterranean diet lifestyle is right here.

Mediterranean Diet Primer

What's fun about a diet? Nothing. Diets may work in the short term to decrease your pant size, but most of the time, they don't benefit your overall health and aren't sustainable over the long haul. People on restrictive diets often gain the weight back after they stop dieting, and some even suffer negative health consequences, such as nutrient deficiencies and slowed metabolism. Wouldn't you rather enjoy life and benefit from the food you eat?

Guess what? The Mediterranean diet is not a "diet" in the typical sense. Rather, it reflects the original meaning of the word *diet*, which is from the Greek language and means "way of life." The Mediterranean diet is a long-term, sustainable way of eating.

One of the reasons this overall eating pattern is consistently voted best overall diet by the *US News & World Report* and other news outlets is because it is not a quick-fix type of diet. It is an eating style that emphasizes delicious, health-promoting foods that are beneficial for a variety of lifestyles, health needs, and goals. The bottom line is that the Mediterranean diet benefits your *overall* health needs, not just your waistline.

A Mediterranean Culture of Eating

The Mediterranean diet is a dietary pattern and lifestyle based on traditional foods found in countries around the Mediterranean Sea. This way of life confers health benefits and may help prevent an array of chronic diseases. In addition to the food itself, this lifestyle focuses on physical movement, taking pleasure in food, and eating socially, as opposed to dining in front of the television.

Although people have been eating this way for hundreds, even thousands of years, the idea of the Mediterranean diet only started back in the 1960s, when the physiologist Ancel Keys first researched this way of eating with the cuisines of Greece and Southern Italy. Today many more countries are included. In fact, the Mediterranean region consists of 22 European, North African, and Middle Eastern countries that border the Mediterranean Sea, so the Mediterranean diet includes an incredible array of cuisines from France, Spain, Italy, Greece, Morocco, Egypt, Turkey, Israel, Syria, Lebanon, and more!

Though these countries have unique cultures and cuisines, they share many commonalities related to food. They all heavily emphasize vegetables, seafood (with less red meat), whole grains, fruit, legumes, nuts, seeds, herbs and spices, and, of course, olive oil. Olive oil is actually the main thread that connects all the Mediterranean regions.

Why It Works

The Mediterranean diet is rich in disease-fighting nutrients.

- **ANTIOXIDANTS.** These powerful compounds protect cells and reduce inflammation to protect us from disease. Antioxidants such as lycopene and polyphenols may even have a protective effect against some cancers.

- **FIBER.** A true super-nutrient, fiber can improve insulin sensitivity, reduce cholesterol and triglycerides, and improve digestion and bowel movements. It is found in foods that typically contain loads of vitamins, minerals, antioxidants, and other health-promoting plant compounds.

- **HEALTHY FATS.** Heart-healthy, plant-based unsaturated fats are emphasized, with extra-virgin olive oil reigning supreme. Omega-3 fatty acids, which are abundant in seafood, play a positive role in brain health as well as heart health. Replacing saturated fat with unsaturated fats from plants and fish may reduce the risk of developing cardiovascular disease.

- **LOWER SODIUM.** Cooking with whole foods that are naturally low in sodium can help reduce blood pressure.

- **VITAMINS AND MINERALS.** Mediterranean foods are especially rich in vitamins C and E, folate, beta-carotene, and selenium, which protect cells from damage, as well as potassium, magnesium, and calcium to help improve blood pressure.

- **WHOLE FOODS.** Minimally processed foods contain all the beneficial nutrients listed here and work in synergy. This means the nutrients have a greater effect in the body because they work together rather than alone.

Why It's Easy

Here's why following the Mediterranean diet is simple and straightforward:

- **BUILT FOR REAL LIFE.** You don't need to follow a specific timeline or super strict rules. The Mediterranean diet gives you a set of suggested guidelines, not a list of stressful restrictions, to help you make long-lasting changes.

- **EVERYDAY HOME COOKING STRATEGIES.** There's no need for fancy cooking equipment or recipes with long ingredient lists. Simple is often better.

- **NO SPECIAL DIET INGREDIENTS OR FAKE SUGARS.** The Mediterranean diet emphasizes minimally processed, whole foods instead of "diet" foods that taste horrible.

Favorite Flavors

The foods of the Mediterranean diet are rich in flavor, and certain ingredients are common across cultures. Signature ingredients that show up throughout Mediterranean countries include tomatoes, peppers, garlic, onion, and lemon—and, of course, olive oil is the common denominator.

The differences in flavors tend to come from the herbs and spices used. For example, although basil and oregano are popular in Italy, North African countries use heavy amounts of parsley and cilantro, and dill is frequently used in Greece. Spanish cuisine often uses smoked paprika, while cinnamon, cumin, and coriander are popular in Moroccan and Turkish cuisine. Sumac, one of my favorite spices and common in Middle Eastern countries, has a bright, lemony taste and is part of the spice blend called za'atar.

North African countries are known for using deliciously intoxicating spice blends containing many components, often with more herbs and spices than you can count on both hands! A few of my favorites are ras el hanout, dukkah, and tabil. If your market sells these spice blends, I recommend picking some up and experimenting with them. They pair very well with meats, poultry, and seafood and are great in stews and soups.

- ◆ **THE PRINCIPLES APPLY TO OTHER TYPES OF GLOBAL CUISINE.** If you don't like certain flavor profiles of the traditional countries represented in this style of eating, no problem. The basic guidelines of the Mediterranean diet can apply to other cuisines around the world, whether you have an affinity for Latin, Asian, or Californian cuisine.

- ◆ **PROMOTES SOCIAL INTERACTION.** When people follow strict diets, it can be too hard to find something to eat at social gatherings, so they often completely give up their social life. Not so for the Mediterranean diet. Social eating in a relaxed atmosphere is encouraged!

Health Benefits

The potential health benefits of the Mediterranean diet are plentiful and well researched. Although not everyone will experience the same results and you may not feel the benefits immediately, remember this is an eating style for long-term health solutions. You'll notice that the health benefits described in this section are all intertwined. The health of one bodily system often affects the health of others. The same nutrients that reduce the risk of one disease often also help reduce the risk of others.

Lower Blood Pressure and Cholesterol

Fruits and vegetables are fantastic sources of potassium, which plays a huge role in improving blood pressure levels. It works by relaxing the blood vessel walls and lessening the effects of sodium. Soluble fiber in plants such as oats, eggplant, apples, chickpeas, flaxseeds, and avocado reduce bad cholesterol by helping it exit the body rather than enter the bloodstream.

Improved Heart Health

Besides lowering blood pressure and cholesterol, improving the health of your blood vessels reduces the risk of heart disease. Powerful nutrients such as omega-3 fatty acids, antioxidants, vitamins, and minerals protect this thin lining, called the endothelium, which in turn helps control blood clotting, lessens inflam-mation, regulates blood pressure, and hinders sticky plaque from developing—all of which may prevent heart attack or stroke. Limiting inflammatory components such as added sugars, refined carbohydrates, saturated fat, and trans fat also has a great impact.

Diabetes Prevention

The Mediterranean diet is not a low-carb lifestyle but instead focuses on healthy carbs that contain high amounts of fiber. Fruits, vegetables, nuts and seeds, whole grains, and legumes all contain fiber, which not only helps stabilize blood sugar levels but also improves overall insulin sensitivity. In avoiding lots of added sugars, the Mediterranean diet also keeps you from experiencing blood sugar spikes.

Improved Gut Health

The gut does more than just digest food and absorb nutrients. In fact, about 70 percent of our immunity resides in the gut. The variety of bacteria in our guts can even influence our weight and our mood. Fiber, the Mediterranean diet super-hero, feeds the good bacteria in the gut, which in turn produces short-chain fatty acids. These end-product fatty acids may even work to prevent common chronic diseases such as type 2 diabetes, heart disease, and obesity.

Reduced Cancer Risk

The large amounts of plant-based foods in the Mediterranean diet are believed to be responsible for a protective effect against cancer. Phytonutrients are powerful compounds found in plants that display anti-inflammatory effects, inhibit the growth of tumors, and fight the destruction of healthy cells. The phytonutrients found in cruciferous veggies, including broccoli, Brussels sprouts, and cabbage, as well as the polyphenols found in extra-virgin olive oil, are particularly potent.

Brain Health

The nutrients in the Mediterranean diet reduce inflammation, help prevent the destruction of healthy brain cells, and even encourage the production of new brain cells, which may slow down the aging process of the brain and protect against cognitive decline. Omega-3 fatty acids from fish may even defend against depression. The additional emphasis on social interaction and physical movement seems to reduce the risk of depression, as well.

Weight Loss

It's important to mention that weight loss reduces the risk of all the diseases in this list. Many research studies show that following a Mediterranean-style eating pattern can help people lose weight. With this approach, you're not focusing on calorie-counting; instead, you're relying on physical movement as well as balanced, minimally processed, whole foods that are healthy and filling.

Lifestyle and Longevity

In addition to the major health benefits described in the previous section, the lifestyle changes associated with the Mediterranean diet can lead to better quality of life, less stress, and more overall enjoyment.

Better Sleep

Emerging research shows that there may be a link between following the Mediterranean diet and better sleep. Although researchers aren't exactly sure why, they think that improvements in health and weight status after following the eating pattern could be the result of several factors. Getting seven to nine hours of quality sleep each night can improve mood, memory and learning, immunity, blood pressure, blood sugar levels, and overall energy levels. It can also lower stress levels and even help control your appetite. When the body does not get enough sleep, the hunger hormones, leptin and ghrelin, get out of whack. The result is increased feelings of hunger and overeating, which may lead to weight gain. If you're always tired, how likely are you to engage in healthy behaviors during the day? Probably not likely.

Activity

Movement is vital to both our mind and body. Exercise through enjoyable movement is an integral part of the Mediterranean diet and is even included as part of the Mediterranean diet pyramid (see Pyramid of Healthy Eating, page 8). Even everyday activities such as walking count as physical activity, but it's important to engage in a variety of types of movement to reap the most reward. Exercise can improve memory and even reduce anxiety, stress, and depression. It also stimulates the brain to grow new neurons and protect existing neurons so we stay mentally sharp, especially as we age. Regular exercise may lower blood pressure, reduce inflammation in the body, and improve cholesterol, all of which protect against heart attack and stroke.

Socializing

The Mediterranean lifestyle encourages eating meals with family and friends rather than alone in front of the television. Research shows that social interaction is good for our mental health. If you have kids, mealtime is a great opportunity to have a conversation and strengthen family relationships. Engaging with others also encourages you to eat more slowly and mindfully instead of at warp speed, which can lead to overeating.

Pyramid of Healthy Eating

The Mediterranean diet food pyramid is a very helpful way to visualize the diet's guidelines. The top level shows the foods that should make up the largest part of our diets: vegetables, fruits, grains (mostly whole grains), olive oil, legumes, nuts, seeds, herbs, and spices. These are all antioxidant-rich ingredients! As we move down, fish and seafood are the main source of non-vegetarian protein. The next level advises you to eat moderate amounts of eggs, poultry, and dairy products like cheese and yogurt. Meat and sweets make up the category you should eat least.

Water should be your main beverage to ensure that you stay hydrated. Red wine is included; however, moderation is key here. That looks like up to one drink per day for women and up to two per day for men. One drink equals a 5-ounce glass of wine. If you don't drink alcohol, though, it's not necessary to start.

Fruits, Vegetables, Grains (mostly whole), Olive oil,
Beans, Nuts, Legumes and Seeds, Herbs and Spices
Base every meal on these foods

Fish and Shellfish
Often, at least two times per week

Poultry, Eggs, Cheese, and Yogurt
Moderate portions,
daily to weekly

Meats and Sweets
Less Often

Wine
In moderation

Water
Drink plenty

Slowing Down

The Mediterranean style of eating focuses on savoring flavors, using local ingredients, and appreciating where your food comes from. Truly savoring your food can help you eat more slowly, with more intention, and listen to your body's fullness cues. In this part of the world, cooking is seen as a pastime and an opportunity to create delicious, nourishing meals that showcase seasonal ingredients. If you're uncertain of how to start, visit your local farmers' markets to learn about what fruits and vegetables are in season.

Mediterranean Diet Principles

Although there aren't any strict rules for the Mediterranean Diet, there is a basic set of guidelines to help steer your food and beverage choices. You won't go wrong if you remember to focus mostly on plant foods, including fruits and veggies, whole grains, nuts and seeds, legumes, and olive oil. Fish is first when it comes to non-plant-based protein, with poultry and meat eaten much less often. Eggs and dairy are eaten in moderation, while added sugars are consumed the least often. Don't forget to hydrate with water and enjoy a glass of red wine if you like.

Fruits and Vegetables

These are the rock stars of the Mediterranean diet. They are low in sodium and rich in minerals like potassium, magnesium, and calcium, which contribute to lower blood pressure. They're also high in fiber, which can help lower cholesterol, prevent constipation, and stabilize blood sugar levels. All produce contain antioxidants, which protect our cells from damage. Different colors contain different types of antioxidants and beneficial plant compounds, so aim to eat a rainbow of fruit and veggie colors. Frozen is just as nutritious as fresh, and you can always use precut veggies to save on prep time.

Whole Grains

No one in Italy would tell you to give up carbs altogether; it's not a realistic or sustainable long-term way of eating. Luckily, you can choose nutrient-dense carbs like starchy vegetables (sweet potatoes, potatoes, corn, butternut squash) and whole grains that are packed with fiber, B vitamins, and antioxidants.

Legumes

Include plant-based proteins such as beans, lentils, chickpeas, edamame, tofu, and tempeh often in your meals. Not only do they add protein to your meal, but they also contain fiber, vitamins, and minerals. Canned legumes are great time-saving ingredients, but be sure to drain and rinse them first to lower the added sodium.

Fish and Shellfish

Focus on omega-3-rich fish and shellfish as your main animal proteins, consuming them at least twice per week. Omega-3 fats are found in seafood such as salmon, sardines, tuna, mackerel, and shrimp. The level of unsafe mercury depends on the type of fish and the water it comes from, so it's best to eat a variety of seafood. Fish with lower mercury levels include salmon, sardines, cod, shrimp, and clams. A great resource to help you choose the most sustainable seafood is the Monterey Bay Aquarium Seafood Watch (SeafoodWatch.org).

Healthy Fats and Oils

The Mediterranean diet is not a low-fat diet, but it is low in saturated fat. The main fat used for cooking and salad dressing is extra-virgin olive oil. Not only is olive oil composed of heart-healthy unsaturated fat, it also contains powerful plant com-pounds called polyphenols that work as antioxidants in the body. Avocados are a source of heart-healthy fat, and they also contain fiber. Nut oils such as sesame, walnut, and pistachio are delicious finishing oils to use for added flavor after cooking.

Dairy and Eggs

Dairy, including cheese, milk, and yogurt, is a rich source of calcium, protein, and vitamin D. Plain Greek yogurt is super versatile and can be used in sweet and savory dishes. It also has the added benefit of containing probiotics, which are good bacteria that have a positive effect on your gut health. Eggs are also a vege-tarian source of protein and vitamin D, the latter being a vitamin found in very few foods. Don't skip the yolks because that's where most of the nutrients are found. Both dairy and eggs contain some saturated fat and are best eaten in moderation.

Lean Meat and Poultry

When consuming meat and poultry, opt for lean cuts and small portions. Think of those proteins as bit players rather than the star of the show. Sirloin, tenderloin, and flank steak are good lean options for beef. Pork loin is also a good option.

Whether you choose white or dark meat poultry, be sure to remove the skin because that is where most of the saturated fat lives. Marinate meats with herbs before grilling to reduce the amount of cancer-causing carcinogens that are produced during the grilling process.

Limited Sweets and Sodium

You should limit added sugars as much as possible, but they're not completely prohibited. A ½-cup serving of gelato as a sweet treat or a small amount of honey or maple syrup in your breakfast yogurt parfait are fine. To limit the amount of salt used in cooking, always taste a dish before adding more salt. Use fresh and dried herbs, spices, chili flakes, and citrus to replace some, or all, of the salt.

Hydration

Water is vital to life. It improves digestion, carries nutrients throughout the body, and protects our organs, to name just a few of its functions. It also prevents dehydration, which can cause headaches, brain fog, dizziness, and sluggishness. Keep a water bottle on your desk as a reminder to sip water throughout the day. Our bodies also get hydration from foods that contain a lot of water, such as fruits and vegetables.

Red Wine

If you already drink alcohol, it's okay to include a glass of red wine with your meal. Red wine contains antioxidants such as resveratrol. But be mindful when drinking and remember that one glass is considered 5 ounces.

Seasonality

Try to choose ingredients that are in season. They often have more flavor because they are at the peak of ripeness. For example, a fresh tomato in the dead of winter won't be nearly as tasty as a vine-ripened tomato at the height of summer. Seasonal ingredients also cost less and are easier to find.

The Mediterranean Kitchen

Keeping a well-stocked kitchen makes following the Mediterranean diet easy. If you have ingredients at your fingertips, you'll be more likely to prepare a delicious home-cooked meal than order out for pizza. When you do go out to a restaurant, keep this list in mind to ensure that you make the best possible choices.

Foods to Reach For

The foods listed here make up the largest part of the Mediterranean diet:

◆ Avocado

◆ Beans, chickpeas, lentils, and dried peas (dried, canned, and frozen)

◆ Condiments such as mustard, hot sauce, and salsa

◆ Extra-virgin olive oil and olives

◆ Fish fillets (fresh or frozen) such as salmon, cod, trout, halibut, tuna, sole, and snapper

◆ Fruit (fresh, frozen, canned in juice, and dried with no added sugar)

◆ Peanut butter and nut butters (unsalted, no added sugar)

◆ Peanuts and nuts (unsalted), such as walnuts, almonds, pistachios, cashews, and pecans

◆ Seafood (canned), including salmon, tuna, and sardines

◆ Seeds, such as sunflower, sesame, pumpkin, flax, chia, and hemp

◆ Shellfish, such as shrimp, clams, mussels, crab, and lobster

◆ Spices, fresh and dried herbs

◆ Vegetables (fresh, frozen, and canned)

◆ Vegetables (jarred, dried, pickled, or fermented), such as sun-dried tomatoes, roasted red peppers, artichoke hearts, and sauerkraut (opt for low-sodium or no-salt added versions whenever possible)

◆ Water

◆ Whole-grain breads, flatbreads, and breakfast cereals

◆ Whole grains such as oats, quinoa, brown rice, farro, wheat berries, bulgur, buckwheat, sorghum, freekeh, and whole-wheat couscous

◆ Whole soy foods such as tofu, tempeh, soy milk, edamame, and soy nuts

Building a Plate

My favorite way to compose a nutritionally balanced meal is by using the plate method. Fill half your plate with vegetables, a quarter with whole grains or starchy vegetables, and a quarter with protein, such as fish or a plant-based source like beans or tofu. You can be an overachiever and make that plate even better by cooking with olive oil, drinking water, and including antioxidant-rich herbs and spices, gut-healthy fermented foods (such as sauerkraut), fiber-rich fruit, and calcium-containing foods (such as almonds, oranges, or Greek yogurt). A balanced plate using recipes from this book, for example, may look like Roasted Chicken with Lemon and Garlic (page 136), Sautéed Zucchini and Shallots with Herbes de Provence (page 57), and Simple Oven-Baked Sweet Potato Fries (page 62).

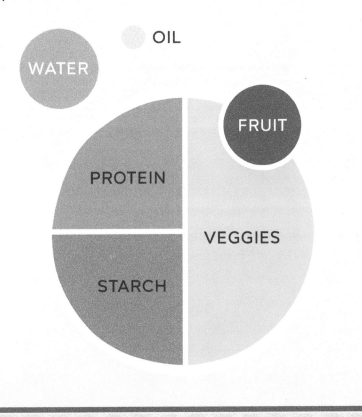

Foods to Moderate

The following foods are still part of the Mediterranean diet, but they're eaten in smaller quantities than the foods listed in in the previous section. There aren't any official guidelines as to specific quantities or portion sizes with the Mediterranean diet; however, the suggestions below from the *Nutrients* journal should give you general guidance.

◆ Beef, pork, and lamb: up to 4 ounces per week

◆ Chicken and turkey: 4 to 8 ounces per week

◆ Dairy, preferably low-fat (such as milk, cottage cheese, and plain Greek yogurt), and cheese (such as feta, mozzarella, and goat cheese): up to 2 cups per day

◆ Eggs (whole), including precooked boiled eggs: up to 4 eggs per week

◆ Refined grains and white pasta: choose whole grains whenever possible, instead

◆ Red wine: in moderation, meaning up to one (5-ounce) drink per day for women and up to two for men (if you don't drink, no need to start)

Foods to Swap

No foods are completely off-limits with the Mediterranean style of eating; however, the following ingredients should be limited as much as possible and make up the smallest part of your diet.

◆ Anything with trans fat

◆ Breakfast foods with excess added sugars, such as Danish, donuts, breakfast cereals, and flavored oatmeal

◆ Butter (swap with olive oil)

◆ Desserts that are high in saturated fat and sugar, such as cakes, pastries, and cookies (swap with fruit-based desserts such as poached pears or baked apples)

◆ Sugar-sweetened beverages such as soda (swap for fruit- or herb-infused water)

◆ Ultra-processed deli meats and hot dogs (when purchasing, look for the shortest ingredient list and lower-sodium options)

◆ Ultra-processed packaged foods containing very high amounts of sodium and additives, such as artificial colors, flavors, and fake sugars

Snacking

Snacks can definitely be part of a healthy diet. (In fact, I included a whole chapter of snacks and small plates on page 37.) When composing a snack, try to include protein, fiber, and a little fat to keep you satiated. Of course, whenever possible, include veggies in your snack. It's easier to get your daily fill of veggies when you eat them throughout the day instead of only at lunch and dinner. Here are some of my favorite simple snacks:

1. Plain Greek yogurt or cottage cheese with berries and chopped nuts

2. Savory Greek yogurt parfait with olive oil, lemon juice, chopped cucumber, and freshly ground black pepper

3. Baby carrots, celery sticks, red pepper strips, and hummus

4. Crispbread topped with Dijon mustard, sliced lower-sodium turkey, and sliced tomato

5. Frozen shelled edamame, quickly thawed in the microwave

6. Beef jerky and air-popped popcorn

7. Whole-wheat toast with ricotta cheese and sliced strawberries

8. Boiled egg, mashed with tahini and fresh dill, served with whole-grain crackers

9. Crispy chickpeas

10. Handful of nuts

11. Whole-wheat tortilla with sliced banana, a tablespoon of natural-style peanut butter, and a sprinkle of cinnamon, warmed in the microwave for 30 seconds

A Lifestyle for the Long Term

What happens when you try to make too many changes all at once? Either you fail immediately or the success is short-lived. I want to give you the tools to make lifestyle changes and health benefits that last a lifetime. One of the best ways to create effective change is to make small adjustments, especially to food choices. Take one small step at a time and keep adding to build on each victory.

Start Small

Here are some simple and actionable changes you can make:

◆ Swap out soda with water.

◆ Jazz up your water by infusing it with fruits and herbs.

◆ Reduce the amount of sugar in your coffee.

◆ Swap out white pasta with whole-wheat or chickpea pasta.

◆ Buy whole-wheat bread instead of white bread.

◆ Choose a handful of nuts instead of potato chips.

◆ Add one veggie, such as spinach, zucchini, or canned pumpkin, to a smoothie.

◆ Eat 2 to 3 cups of veggies daily.

◆ Add beans, lentils, or chickpeas to your diet each day, even if that means starting out with just a few tablespoons.

◆ Swap out butter with olive oil when cooking.

◆ Eat fruit for dessert.

◆ Choose a handful of dark chocolate chips (at least 70 percent cacao) instead of pastries and cookies.

◆ Remove the saltshaker from the table.

◆ Use less salt when cooking by seasoning food with lemon, oregano, smoked paprika, and chili flakes.

Get Active

You don't need to compete in a marathon to reap the benefits of exercise. All movement counts, including seemingly simple activities like taking a brisk walk around the block, mowing the lawn, or dancing in your living room. The key is to move often throughout the day and not stay stagnant at your desk or on the couch.

The Mediterranean lifestyle emphasizes walking, which is a fantastic way to move your body, especially if you are just starting to exercise. The CDC recommends 150 minutes of moderate-intensity movement each week, which could translate into 30 minutes of walking five days a week. You don't need to get all of your walking in at once. All those steps you take throughout the day count, even if it's just for 10 minutes at a time. Buy a good pair of sneakers and walk to shops, use the stairs whenever possible, and take a brisk stroll on your lunch break.

The best way to start an exercise routine and keep yourself engaged is to pick an activity that you enjoy. If you like riding your bike, taking a yoga class, or swimming, you're more likely to turn those activities into habits.

Improve Sleep

When we sleep, our bodies recover and recharge. Try out these suggestions to improve the quality of your sleep.

◆ Don't drink caffeinated beverages after lunchtime.

◆ Don't drink alcohol right before bedtime. Although it may seem like booze will help you fall asleep, it wreaks havoc on your quality of sleep.

◆ Stop eating two to three hours before bedtime.

◆ Incorporate sleep-promoting foods and beverages at evening meals, such as almonds, walnuts, kiwifruit, salmon, tart cherry juice, and chamomile tea.

◆ Limit screen time before bed and silence the ringer on your cell phone.

◆ Purchase nice sheets that feel good on your skin and pillows that properly support your neck.

◆ Practice meditation right before bed to calm your mind.

◆ Listen to soft nature music to help you fall asleep.

◆ Keep the room temperature around 65°F.

◆ Make sure your room is dark enough.

◆ Make it a habit to go to bed at a regular time each night.

About the Recipes

If you're anything like me, the last thing you want to do is spend all day in the kitchen. The point of the recipes in this book is to make practicing a healthy way of eating easy, fast, and, of course, delicious, with tasty Mediterranean flavors. I have included cooking labels and tips to streamline recipe selection and execution.

You'll notice that each recipe has a set of dietary labels indicating if the recipe is gluten-free, dairy-free, nut-free, vegan, or vegetarian. I also included labels to indicate different types of preparation. Every single recipe is labeled with at least one, but many have more.

- **BIG-BATCH:** These recipes make six or more servings and freeze well. Perfect to help you meal-plan for those days when all you want to do is heat and serve. Stuffed Bell Peppers with Quinoa, Kidney Beans, and Mozzarella (page 84) freeze very well.

- **15-MINUTE:** From start to finish, including prep, these recipes are done in only 15 minutes. Check out the Tuna-Stuffed Avocados (page 125). Delicious!

- **5-INGREDIENT:** Each recipe contains only five ingredients or fewer, not counting salt, black pepper, oil, and water. Balsamic Strawberries with Whipped Vanilla Ricotta (page 158) is one of my favorite sweet treats!

- **NO-COOK:** Absolutely no heat source is required to make these recipes. Raspberry-Kefir Smoothie (page 27) is a super easy breakfast.

- **ONE-POT:** These recipes are cooked entirely in one pot or pan (e.g., a Dutch oven, 12-inch skillet, or sheet pan), which means fewer dishes to wash. I love easy sheet pan meals, like the Greek-Inspired Veggie and Chickpea Sheet Pan Meal (page 86).

- **30-MINUTE:** For when you have a little more time, these recipes take no more than 30 minutes from start to finish. Mediterranean Steak Bowl with Bulgur, Hummus, and Feta (page 148) is a complete meal in only half an hour.

Most of the recipes also include useful **TIPS** to help you out in the kitchen:

- **COOKING TIP:** Helpful information that may make the dish easier and faster to prep, cook, or clean up.

- **INGREDIENT TIP:** These tips will give you more info on selecting and buying ingredients, working with them, and making substitutions when applicable. I'll also give you surprising and helpful nutrition facts, as well as some suggestions on swapping out ingredients for dietary reasons such as food allergies.

◆ **STORAGE TIP:** Even when stored at safe temperatures, food can only keep its quality for so long. I'll give you helpful time ranges for storing your food in the refrigerator and freezer for the highest level of freshness.

◆ **VARIATION TIP:** These tips include suggestions for adding or changing ingredients and cooking methods to mix things up and make the recipe your own.

Green Shakshuka, *page 31*

Breakfast and Brunch

PREP TIME:
5 minutes

COOK TIME:
20 minutes

MAKES
16 COOKIES

Banana-Almond Breakfast Cookies

If you need breakfast on the go, this recipe is for you! Don't let the size of these cookies fool you. Because they are full of heart-healthy almond butter and whole-grain oats, they land solidly in the Mediterranean diet, and they are filling. Grab a couple on your way out the door and munch on them in the car or at your desk. They're also great as an afternoon snack.

Nonstick cooking spray

2 ripe medium bananas

1 cup unsalted, unsweetened creamy almond butter

2 cups rolled oats

1 teaspoon vanilla extract

2 tablespoons pure maple syrup

1. Preheat the oven to 350°F. Line a sheet pan with a silicone baking mat or parchment paper and lightly coat with cooking spray.

2. In a medium bowl, mash the bananas. Add the almond butter, oats, vanilla extract, and maple syrup and stir until combined.

3. Scoop 16 heaping tablespoons onto the sheet pan. If you have extra dough left in the bowl, divide it among the mounds. Slightly flatten each mound.

4. Bake for 20 minutes, or until the cookies are golden brown. Let cool on a wire rack.

STORAGE TIP: These cookies last in the freezer for up to 3 months. After baking and cooling, place the cookies in an airtight container. To thaw, remove them from the freezer and defrost, either in the refrigerator or at room temperature.

PER SERVING: Calories: 154; Total fat: 9g; Saturated fat: 1g; Sodium: 2g; Total carbohydrates: 15g; Sugar: 4g; Fiber: 3g; Protein: 5g; Calcium: 63mg

Apple-Cinnamon Quinoa Porridge

DAIRY-FREE
GLUTEN-FREE
ONE-POT
30-MINUTE
VEGAN

PREP TIME:
5 minutes

COOK TIME:
15 minutes

SERVES 4

I love oatmeal, but sometimes I want to change things up for breakfast. Quinoa is technically a seed, but nutritionally it's categorized as a whole grain, and it contains about 8 grams of protein per cup. It's a good idea to rinse the quinoa before cooking to remove any bitter-tasting compounds called saponins. However, some quinoa is sold pre-rinsed, which will save you a step, so check the package. Also, if you're avoiding gluten, check the soy milk carton to be sure none of the added ingredients contains gluten.

¾ cup quinoa, rinsed
¾ teaspoon ground cinnamon
Pinch ground nutmeg
Pinch ground cloves
1¾ cups unsweetened soy milk
1 teaspoon vanilla extract

1 tablespoon pure maple syrup
2 small green apples, cut into 1-inch pieces
¼ cup shelled pistachios, whole or pieces

1. In a saucepan over high heat, combine the quinoa, cinnamon, nutmeg, cloves, and soy milk and bring to a boil. Lower the heat to very low and simmer for 7 minutes, stirring occasionally. Be sure to keep your eye on the pot to make sure the liquid stays at a simmer.

2. Add the apples, stir, and continue simmering until the quinoa looks creamy, about 7 minutes. Add the vanilla extract and maple syrup. It's okay if the mixture still looks a little soupy. It will thicken as it cools.

3. Spoon the porridge into four bowls and top each with 1 tablespoon of pistachios. Serve warm.

COOKING TIP: Leftover porridge reheats very well the next day. Add a splash of your desired milk to moisten, then heat in the microwave until hot. Garnish with the pistachios just before serving.

PER SERVING: Calories: 289; Total fat: 8g; Saturated fat: 1g; Sodium: 48g; Total carbohydrates: 44g; Sugar: 12g; Fiber: 7g; Protein: 11g; Calcium: 175mg

PREP TIME:
15 minutes

COOK TIME:
40 minutes

SERVES 8

Blueberry, Lemon Zest, and Almond Baked Oatmeal

This oatmeal bake is packed with potent, anti-inflammatory antioxidants from the blueberries, flaxseed, lemon zest, oats, olive oil, and almonds, which is what the Mediterranean diet is all about. For even more antioxidants and flavor, add ground cinnamon, ginger, or cardamom. I used soy milk for this recipe, but feel free to use any other unsweetened plant-based beverage or cow's milk instead.

Nonstick cooking spray or olive oil, for greasing
12 ounces frozen blueberries, not thawed
3 cups rolled oats
1 teaspoon baking powder
3 tablespoons ground flaxseed

Zest of 2 lemons
2 eggs
¼ cup olive oil
1½ cups unsweetened vanilla soy milk
⅓ cup pure maple syrup
½ cup slivered almonds

1. Preheat the oven to 350°F. Spray an 8-by-11-inch (2-quart) baking dish with cooking spray or brush with oil.

2. In a large bowl, mix together the blueberries, oats, baking powder, flaxseed, lemon zest, eggs, oil, soy milk, and maple syrup. Pour the mixture into the prepared baking dish.

3. Sprinkle the slivered almonds evenly across the top of the oatmeal and bake for 40 minutes.

4. Serve warm.

STORAGE TIP: Cover with plastic wrap or aluminum foil and refrigerate for up to 6 days or freeze for up to 6 months. Reheat in the microwave.

PER SERVING: Calories: 321; Total fat: 16g; Saturated fat: 2g; Sodium: 40g; Total carbohydrates: 38g; Sugar: 12g; Fiber: 6g; Protein: 9g; Calcium: 388mg

Orange-Scented Cherry Yogurt Parfait

15-MINUTE
5-INGREDIENT
GLUTEN-FREE
NO-COOK
NUT-FREE
VEGETARIAN

PREP TIME:
10 minutes

SERVES 2

I love the flavor combination of cherry and orange. A great benefit of using frozen cherries is that they produce deliciously sweet juice when they defrost. Not only does the orange zest add a pop of flavor, but it is also rich in bioactive compounds called phytochemicals that offer anti-inflammatory, free radical–fighting, and even antitumor health benefits.

1 cup low-fat (2 percent) plain Greek yogurt
Zest and juice of 1 orange
½ teaspoon honey

⅔ cup frozen cherries, thawed in the refrigerator
¼ cup raw green pumpkin seeds (also sold as pepitas)

1. In a medium bowl, mix together the yogurt, orange zest, 2 tablespoons of orange juice, and honey until well combined.

2. Place ½ cup of yogurt into each of two small bowls. Top each mound of yogurt with ⅓ cup of thawed cherries and 2 tablespoons of pumpkin seeds. Spoon any remaining cherry juice over the parfaits. Serve immediately.

INGREDIENT TIP: If you have leftover orange juice, pour it into an ice cube tray and freeze. Defrost when you're ready to make this parfait the next time or add the orange ice cubes to drinking water for a flavor boost.

PER SERVING: Calories: 223; Total fat: 9g; Saturated fat: 2g; Sodium: 38g; Total carbohydrates: 19g; Sugar: 14g; Fiber: 2g; Protein: 17g; Calcium: 137mg

Peach, Cinnamon, and Walnut Overnight Oats

Overnight oats are one of the easiest, healthiest, and most satisfying make-ahead breakfasts. They are also versatile because you have the option of eating them cold or heating them up. Because peaches are seasonal, using frozen peaches allows you to enjoy summer fruit all year long. If you don't like peaches, switch them out for any fruit you like.

1⅓ cups rolled oats
2½ cups unsweetened vanilla soy milk
3 tablespoons chia seeds
½ teaspoon ground cinnamon

2 tablespoons pure maple syrup
1 teaspoon lemon juice
½ cup walnut pieces
2 cups roughly chopped frozen or fresh peaches

1. In a large bowl, mix together the oats, soy milk, chia seeds, cinnamon, maple syrup, lemon juice, walnuts, and peaches.

2. Cover the bowl and refrigerate for at least 4 hours or overnight. Alternatively, you can divide the oat mixture among four individual containers or mason jars and refrigerate.

3. Serve cold, or warm it up in the microwave to your desired temperature.

INGREDIENT TIP: If you follow a gluten-free diet, be sure to use certified gluten-free oats.

PER SERVING: Calories: 340; Total fat: 15g; Saturated fat: 2g; Sodium: 59g; Total carbohydrates: 40g; Sugar: 12g; Fiber: 9g; Protein: 12g; Calcium: 294mg

Raspberry-Kefir Smoothie

15-MINUTE
5-INGREDIENT
GLUTEN-FREE
NO-COOK
NUT-FREE
VEGETARIAN

PREP TIME:
10 minutes

SERVES 2

The tanginess of this smoothie comes from a drinkable yogurt beverage called kefir, which actually contains more probiotics than yogurt. I recommend using plain kefir because it does not contain added sugar, unlike many flavored versions. You'll notice that zucchini is also an ingredient, but it is so mildly flavored, you won't even taste it!

1½ cups low-fat (1 percent) plain, unsweetened kefir

1¼ cups frozen raspberries

1 ripe medium banana

¾ cup coarsely chopped zucchini

2 teaspoons honey

In a blender, combine the kefir, raspberries, banana, zucchini, and honey and blend until smooth. Taste, and adjust the amount of honey, if desired. Pour the mixture into two glasses and serve.

VARIATION TIP: Try using the same amount of spinach or cauliflower, which are also mild-flavored, instead of the zucchini.

PER SERVING: Calories: 261; Total fat: 3g; Saturated fat: 1g; Sodium: 101g; Total carbohydrates: 53g; Sugar: 34g; Fiber: 9g; Protein: 11g; Calcium: 329mg

15-MINUTE
NO-COOK
NUT-FREE
VEGETARIAN

PREP TIME:
10 minutes

SERVES 2

Breakfast Mezze Plate

Breakfast in the eastern Mediterranean often includes veggies like cucumbers, tomatoes, olives, hummus, and flatbread. Nothing like our Western-style breakfasts! This is super simple to throw together and especially great if you tend to crave a savory morning meal.

6 radishes, quartered
  or halved

⅔ cup sliced English or
  Persian cucumber

8 cherry tomatoes, halved

8 small green olives

¼ cup Lemony Parsley
  Hummus (page 44) or
  store-bought hummus

2 hard-boiled eggs, halved

2 whole-wheat pitas, each cut
  into 4 pieces

Divide the radish, cucumber, tomatoes, olives, hummus, egg, and pita between two plates. Serve and enjoy at room temperature.

INGREDIENT TIP: To hard-boil eggs, place them in a saucepan, cover with water, and bring to a boil over medium-high heat. As soon as the water starts to boil, place a lid on the pan and turn off the heat. Set a timer for 12 minutes. When the timer goes off, drain the hot water and run cold water over the eggs. Peel them when cool.

PER SERVING: Calories: 336; Total fat: 10g; Saturated fat: 2g; Sodium: 705g; Total carbohydrates: 47g; Sugar: 4g; Fiber: 7g; Protein: 15g; Calcium: 76mg

Leek, Zucchini, and Prosciutto Frittata

GLUTEN-FREE
NUT-FREE
30-MINUTE

PREP TIME:
10 minutes

COOK TIME:
20 minutes

SERVES 6

An open-faced Italian-style omelet, known as a frittata, is great for breakfast, brunch, or even a light lunch or dinner. I like to serve this frittata with a side of fruit at morning meals or a simple green salad when eaten later in the day. If you have any leftover cooked grains such as rice or quinoa, place a layer of the grain on top of the sautéed vegetables before pouring the egg over the top.

2 teaspoons olive oil

1 large leek, white and light green parts, cut in half lengthwise, then cut into half-moons

1 large zucchini, halved lengthwise and cut into half-moons

8 large eggs

½ cup low-fat (1 percent) milk

½ teaspoon garlic powder

½ cup shredded Gruyère or Swiss cheese

2 ounces prosciutto (about 4 slices)

1. Preheat the oven to 375°F.

2. Heat the oil in a 10-inch oven-safe nonstick skillet over medium-high heat, until the oil is shimmering. Add the sliced leeks and cook, stirring occasionally, for 2 minutes.

3. Add the zucchini and cook for another 3 minutes.

4. While the veggies cook, in a large bowl, beat together the eggs, milk, and garlic powder until slightly frothy. Add the shredded cheese and stir until combined.

5. Add the prosciutto to the veggies and stir until evenly distrib-uted. Remove the pan from the heat, pour the egg mixture into the pan, and bake for 18 to 20 minutes, or until the eggs are set.

Recipe continued →

6. When the handle of the pan is cool enough to handle, run a rubber spatula along the edge of the frittata to loosen it. Place a large dinner plate over the frittata and flip the pan over. The frittata should come loose from the pan and onto the plate.

7. Cut the frittata into 6 slices and serve warm.

INGREDIENT TIP: The best lower-sodium cheese I have found is the shredded Swiss and Gruyère blend from Trader Joe's. It's full of flavor but has about half the amount of sodium of Cheddar cheese.

PER SERVING: Calories: 202; Total fat: 13g; Saturated fat: 5g; Sodium: 382g; Total carbohydrates: 6g; Sugar: 3g; Fiber: 1g; Protein: 15g; Calcium: 168mg

Green Shakshuka

Shakshuka is a popular egg dish in countries such as Israel, Tunisia, and Egypt. The eggs are traditionally simmered in tomato sauce, but this version uses sautéed green veggies as a hearty base instead. I recommend serving this delicious meal with whole-wheat pita bread.

GLUTEN-FREE
NUT-FREE
ONE-POT
30-MINUTE
VEGETARIAN

PREP TIME:
10 minutes

COOK TIME:
15 minutes

SERVES 3

1 tablespoon olive oil

1½ cups thinly sliced Brussels sprouts

1 bunch scallions, white and green parts, thinly sliced

2 teaspoons chopped garlic

2 cups frozen chopped spinach, thawed (do not squeeze out liquid)

½ teaspoon dried oregano

¼ teaspoon coarse kosher salt

½ cup packed marinated artichoke heart quarters, drained

3 large eggs

Optional toppings: crumbled soft goat cheese, chopped scallions, and tomato wedges

1. Heat the oil in a 12-inch nonstick skillet over medium heat, until the oil is shimmering. Add the Brussels sprouts, scallions, and garlic and cook, stirring occasionally, for 3 minutes.

2. Add the spinach, oregano, and salt, and cook for another 3 minutes. Add the artichoke hearts and stir until combined.

3. Make 4 wells in the spinach mixture. Break an egg into a drinking glass and pour it into one of the wells in the pan. Repeat with the remaining 3 eggs.

4. Cover the pan, lower the heat to medium-low, and cook until the eggs are set, 6 to 8 minutes. Sprinkle with the goat cheese and scallions and serve warm with tomato wedges (if using).

PER SERVING: Calories: 221; Total fat: 14g; Saturated fat: 4g; Sodium: 489g; Total carbohydrates: 14g; Sugar: 3g; Fiber: 6g; Protein: 13g; Calcium: 209mg

Savory Cottage Cheese with Cucumber and Sumac

Savory yogurt parfaits are one of my favorite breakfasts, so it made sense to do the same with cottage cheese. Sumac is a popular ground spice in Middle Eastern cuisine and imparts a lovely subtle lemony flavor. You should be able to find it at major supermarkets under brand names such as Spicely Organics, Sadaf, Morton & Bassett, and Ziyad. If you need to watch sodium intake, look for a low-sodium or no-salt-added cottage cheese.

1½ cups chopped English or
   Persian cucumber
2 teaspoons olive oil
1 teaspoon ground sumac

2 tablespoons chopped
   fresh chives
1½ cups low-fat (2 percent)
   cottage cheese
2 tablespoons walnut pieces

1. In a small bowl, mix together the cucumber, oil, sumac, and chives.

2. Place ¾ cup of cottage cheese into each of two bowls and divide the cucumber mixture between the bowls.

3. Sprinkle 1 tablespoon of walnuts over each bowl and serve.

INGREDIENT TIP: Sumac can be rubbed on seafood and lamb chops, mixed into salad dressings, roasted with chickpeas, and even sprinkled on top of hummus. If you can't find sumac, try mixing the zest of 1 lemon with the cucumbers to get that lemony taste. If you like heat, add black pepper or red chili flakes.

PER SERVING: Calories: 238; Total fat: 14g; Saturated fat: 3g; Sodium: 562g; Total carbohydrates: 12g; Sugar: 8g; Fiber: 1g; Protein: 20g; Calcium: 211mg

Scrambled Eggs with Spinach and Feta

15-MINUTE
5-INGREDIENT
GLUTEN-FREE
NUT-FREE
VEGETARIAN

PREP TIME:
5 minutes

COOK TIME:
5 minutes

SERVES 4

In a Mediterranean diet, it is ideal to eat veggies throughout the day instead of trying to have them all at lunch and dinner. Eggs are a fantastic vehicle for adding all types of veggies, including spinach, broccoli, zucchini, kale, and arugula—or the favorite in my household, caramelized onions and red bell peppers. Chopped fresh herbs such as dill, chives, or basil would be delicious, too. The possibilities are nearly endless.

8 large eggs
Pinch freshly ground
   black pepper
2 teaspoons olive oil

1 (5-ounce) package baby
   spinach leaves
½ cup crumbled feta cheese
Hot sauce, such as Tabasco,
   for serving (optional)

1. In a medium bowl, whisk together the eggs and black pepper.

2. Heat the oil in a 12-inch nonstick skillet over medium heat until the oil is shimmering. Add the spinach and cook until wilted, about 1 minute.

3. Add the beaten eggs to the skillet and cook until the eggs start to set on the sides of the pan. Stir to scramble and continue cooking and stirring until eggs are set, about 2 minutes.

4. Stir in the feta cheese and serve immediately, with hot sauce (if using).

INGREDIENT TIP: When I need to bulk up the portion size of scrambled eggs for bigger eaters without adding more saturated fat, I add liquid egg whites to my whole eggs. Three tablespoons of egg whites are equivalent to 1 large whole egg.

PER SERVING: Calories: 218; Total fat: 16g; Saturated fat: 6g; Sodium: 485g; Total carbohydrates: 2g; Sugar: 1g; Fiber: 1g; Protein: 16g; Calcium: 179mg

Smoked Trout, Avocado, and Arugula Naan with Dill Yogurt

Trout is an unappreciated fish. It's one of the healthiest sea-food options and a rich source of omega-3 fatty acids. Plus, it's delicious! If your store doesn't carry smoked trout, hot or cold smoked salmon would be a nice alternative.

2 (4-ounce) pieces whole-grain naan (such as Stonefire brand)

1 cup low-fat (2 percent) plain Greek yogurt

2 teaspoons lemon juice

¼ cup chopped fresh dill

1 tablespoon olive oil

⅛ teaspoon coarse kosher salt

4 ounces smoked trout, skin removed, flesh flaked (3 ounces if the trout comes skinless)

½ avocado, thinly sliced

1 cup packed baby arugula

1. Preheat the oven to 400°F.

2. Place the naan on a sheet pan and bake for 7 minutes or until the flatbread is just starting to crisp.

3. While the naan is toasting, in a small bowl, mix together the yogurt, lemon, dill, oil, and salt.

4. Place the toasted naan on a cutting board.

5. Spread ½ cup of the yogurt mixture over each piece of naan. Evenly place the trout and avocado slices over the yogurt. Top with the arugula.

6. Cut each piece of naan in half and serve immediately.

VARIATION TIP: To take this flatbread over the top, add a layer of scrambled eggs over the yogurt, then add the fish, avocado, and arugula on top.

PER SERVING: Calories: 331; Total fat: 14g; Saturated fat: 2g; Sodium: 708g; Total carbohydrates: 35g; Sugar: 6g; Fiber: 5g; Protein: 17g; Calcium: 141mg

Lemony Parsley Hummus, *page 44*

Snacks and Small Plates

PREP TIME:
10 minutes,
plus
20 minutes
to chill

SERVES 6

Apricot and Almond Oat Bites

I always keep a batch of energy bites on hand in the freezer. They are a super satisfying snack, quick to make, and handy to take on the go. They're great for breakfast or a sweet treat. Hemp seeds are a nutritious addition, containing plant-based omega-3 fatty acids, protein, vitamin E, and magnesium—all nutrients common to foods around the Mediterranean. If your store doesn't carry hemp seeds, you can use ground flaxseeds, often sold as flax meal.

½ cup unsalted, unsweet-
   ened almond butter
½ cup rolled oats
⅓ cup chopped dried apricots
1 tablespoon maple syrup

3 tablespoons hemp seeds
½ teaspoon ground
   cinnamon
2 tablespoons coarsely
   chopped slivered almonds

1. In a medium bowl, mix together the almond butter, oats, apricots, maple syrup, hemp seeds, cinnamon, and almonds.

2. Form the mixture into 12 balls, slightly smaller than a golf ball, and place them on a plate. Freeze for 20 minutes, until they firm up.

3. Enjoy chilled or at room temperature.

STORAGE TIP: The bites may be stored in an airtight container in the refrigerator for up to 5 days or frozen for up to 3 months.

PER SERVING (2 BALLS): Calories: 209; Total fat: 15g; Saturated fat: 1g; Sodium: 2g; Total carbohydrates: 13g; Sugar: 4g; Fiber: 4g; Protein: 8g; Calcium: 162mg

Warm Garlic Olives

I love heart-healthy olives, but they're even better when warmed with a garlic-and-herb-infused oil. I highly recommend serving a few slices of baguette alongside to sop up the flavorful oil and caramelized garlic slices. You can use any black or green olive, but don't use standard canned black olives.

DAIRY-FREE
15-MINUTE
5-INGREDIENT
GLUTEN-FREE
NUT-FREE
VEGAN

PREP TIME:
5 minutes

COOK TIME:
10 minutes

SERVES 4

1 orange
2 tablespoons olive oil
4 garlic cloves, thinly sliced
4 thyme sprigs
½ cup pitted Manzanilla olives

½ cup pitted Kalamata olives
Pinch freshly ground
 black pepper
Sliced baguette, for serving
 (optional)

1. Preheat the oven to 400°F.

2. Using a peeler, remove 4 large pieces of peel from the orange. Squeeze 2 tablespoons of juice from the orange.

3. Heat the oil, garlic, and thyme sprigs in an oven-safe 10-inch skillet over medium-low heat. Let the aromatics infuse the oil for 2 minutes.

4. Add the olives, orange peel, and orange juice to the pan and stir until combined. Bake the olives for 8 minutes. Sprinkle the pepper over the olives and spoon everything from the pan into a serving bowl. Serve warm with the bread slices (if using).

PER SERVING: Calories: 158; Total fat: 16g; Saturated fat: 2g; Sodium: 444g; Total carbohydrates: 4g; Sugar: 1g; Fiber: 1g; Protein: 2g; Calcium: 7mg

PREP TIME:
5 minutes

COOK TIME:
30 minutes

SERVES 3

Roasted Garlic and Dill Chickpeas

What's just as delicious and addictive to snack on as chips? Roasted chickpeas! Luckily, chickpeas, a plentiful legume around the Mediterranean, are much healthier than chips and pack a protein and fiber punch to keep us fuller longer. They make the perfect snack, and you can also add them to salads in place of croutons. Removing excess water from the chickpeas and cooking them on an unlined sheet pan help ensure a crispy result.

1 (15-ounce) can low-sodium chickpeas, drained and rinsed
1 tablespoon plus 1 teaspoon olive oil

¼ teaspoon coarse kosher salt
1 teaspoon garlic powder
1 teaspoon onion powder
2 teaspoons dried dill
¾ teaspoon mustard powder

1. Preheat the oven to 400°F.

2. Place a clean dish towel on an unlined sheet pan and place the chickpeas on top, blotting them well with the towel. Discard any skins that have come off. Remove the towel and toss the chickpeas with the oil and salt on the pan.

3. Roast for 20 to 30 minutes, shaking the pan every 10 minutes, until they are golden and crispy. They will also get slightly crispier as they cool.

4. In a medium bowl, mix together the garlic powder, onion powder, dill, and mustard. Add the chickpeas and toss until evenly coated.

5. Serve immediately.

STORAGE TIP: Although the crispness of the chickpeas goes away fairly quickly, they're still tasty for a few days when stored in an airtight container at room temperature.

PER SERVING: Calories: 169; Total fat: 9g; Saturated fat: 1g; Sodium: 349g; Total carbohydrates: 19g; Sugar: 3g; Fiber: 5g; Protein: 6g; Calcium: 57mg

Spice-Roasted Almonds

Jazz up plain almonds by warming them in the oven with a mixture of olive oil and spices. It's as simple as that. Just be sure to grab a napkin because your fingers will get messy! Almonds are nutritional powerhouses, packed with vitamin E, magnesium, and fiber. Don't use blanched almonds because most of the antioxidants are in the brown skins.

DAIRY-FREE
15-MINUTE
GLUTEN-FREE
ONE-POT
VEGAN

PREP TIME:
5 minutes

COOK TIME:
10 minutes

SERVES 4

1 teaspoon chili powder
1 teaspoon paprika
½ teaspoon ground coriander
½ teaspoon ground cumin

¼ teaspoon ground cinnamon
¼ teaspoon coarse kosher salt
1 cup whole raw almonds
2 teaspoons olive oil

1. Preheat the oven to 350°F. Line a sheet pan with a silicone baking mat or parchment paper.

2. In a small bowl, mix together the chili powder, paprika, coriander, cumin, cinnamon, and salt. Place the almonds on sheet pan, add the spice mixture and the oil, and toss until evenly coated.

3. Bake for 5 minutes. Shake the pan and continue baking for 3 minutes, or until the spices have darkened in color, but aren't burnt.

4. Serve warm or at room temperature.

STORAGE TIP: Place the almonds in an airtight container and store at room temperature for up to 5 days.

PER SERVING: Calories: 234; Total fat: 21g; Saturated fat: 2g; Sodium: 79g; Total carbohydrates: 9g; Sugar: 2g; Fiber: 5g; Protein: 8g; Calcium: 104mg

PREP TIME:
15 minutes

COOK TIME:
5 minutes

SERVES 4

Tomato and Garlic Bruschetta

If you are a garlic lover, you need to make this recipe, but not for a first date! Be sure to use ripe in-season tomatoes to get the best flavor. Some people add either balsamic or red wine vinegar as well, but I like the simple taste of the garlic, tomatoes, olive oil, and basil. If you have time, allow the bruschetta to sit for 30 minutes, and the flavors will continue to blend. Garnish with sharp Parmesan cheese, if desired.

15 ounces vine-ripened tomatoes, cored and chopped
1½ teaspoons minced garlic
2 tablespoons olive oil, divided
¼ cup chopped fresh basil
¼ teaspoon coarse kosher salt

Pinch freshly ground black pepper
Pinch red chili flakes
4 ounces French baguette, cut into 24 (¼-inch-thick) slices
Grated Parmesan cheese, for garnish (optional)

1. Preheat the oven to 350°F.

2. In a medium bowl, mix together the tomatoes, garlic, 1 tablespoon of oil, basil, salt, pepper, and chili flakes.

3. Place the baguette slices on a sheet pan and brush with the remaining 1 tablespoon of oil. Bake for 5 minutes, or until the bread is toasted.

4. Place 1 tablespoon of bruschetta on top of each bread slice, garnish with the Parmesan cheese (if using), and serve.

COOKING TIP: An 8-inch serrated knife makes it so easy to slice a crusty loaf of bread, and a serrated paring knife makes cutting tomatoes a breeze. I highly recommend having these two types of knives in your kitchen.

PER SERVING: Calories: 147; Total fat: 8g; Saturated fat: 1g; Sodium: 314g; Total carbohydrates: 18g; Sugar: 3g; Fiber: 2g; Protein: 3g; Calcium: 19mg

Avocado Dip with Pepitas and Pomegranate Seeds

DAIRY-FREE
15-MINUTE
GLUTEN-FREE
NO-COOK
NUT-FREE
VEGAN

PREP TIME:
10 minutes

SERVES 4

You might be thinking that this recipe sounds a lot like guaca-mole, which is traditionally a Latin dish, but it fits perfectly into a Mediterranean Diet with its heart-healthy fat and fresh herbs and spices. I added the pumpkin seeds for crunch and the pomegranate for a touch of tangy sweetness. When selecting your crudités (cut-up raw vegetables), use a variety of crunchy sliced veggies such as cucumber, jicama, carrots, celery, or radish.

1 cup mashed avocado
½ teaspoon garlic powder
1½ teaspoons lime juice
¼ cup chopped fresh cilantro
Few dashes hot sauce, such as Tabasco
¼ teaspoon coarse kosher salt

2 tablespoons raw green pumpkin seeds (also sold as pepitas)
3 tablespoons pomegranate seeds
Vegetable crudité of choice, for serving

1. In a small bowl, mix together the mashed avocado, garlic powder, lime juice, cilantro, hot sauce, and salt.

2. Transfer the avocado mixture to a serving bowl and top with the pumpkin seeds and pomegranate seeds.

3. Arrange the vegetables on a platter and serve with the dip.

INGREDIENT TIP: If you have a nut allergy, pepitas are a flavorful substitute in recipes that call for nuts. If you have a couple of extra minutes, toast them in a dry skillet for extra flavor.

PER SERVING: Calories: 120; Total fat: 10g; Saturated fat: 2g; Sodium: 90g; Total carbohydrates: 8g; Sugar: 2g; Fiber: 4g; Protein: 3g; Calcium: 9mg

Lemony Parsley Hummus

Homemade hummus is so easy to make and so delicious, you may never buy it again. A staple in Mediterranean cuisine, it's popular in places such as Israel, Greece, Egypt, Turkey, Palestine, Cyprus, and more. Although various regions add different ingredients, the main items used are always chickpeas, tahini, lemon juice, garlic, and olive oil.

PREP TIME:
10 minutes

MAKES
1½ CUPS

1 (15-ounce) can low-sodium chickpeas, drained and rinsed
1 cup chopped fresh parsley
¼ cup unsalted tahini
½ teaspoon chopped garlic

¼ cup lemon juice
½ teaspoon coarse kosher salt
3 tablespoons olive oil, plus 1 teaspoon
3 tablespoons cold water

1. In a food processor, combine the chickpeas, parsley, tahini, garlic, lemon juice, salt, 3 tablespoons of oil, and cold water and blend until smooth.

2. Taste and adjust the seasonings, if desired, then drizzle the remaining 1 teaspoon of oil over the top of the hummus.

VARIATION TIP: To add a wow factor to your hummus, sprinkle za'atar, a Middle Eastern spice mix of dried thyme leaves, sumac, and sesame, in addition to a small handful of pine nuts, over the top.

PER SERVING (¼ CUP): Calories: 168; Total fat: 14g; Saturated fat: 2g; Sodium: 197g; Total carbohydrates: 10g; Sugar: 1g; Fiber: 3g; Protein: 4g; Calcium: 37mg

Whole-Wheat Pita Chips

Besides being super simple, making your own pita chips is a great way to use up pita bread that might be a bit stale. You can use the chips for dipping or throw them into salads in place of croutons. Feel free to switch around the seasonings and use spices such as cumin, coriander, sumac, or cayenne.

DAIRY-FREE
15-MINUTE
5-INGREDIENT
NUT-FREE
ONE-POT
VEGETARIAN

PREP TIME:
5 minutes

COOK TIME:
10 minutes

MAKES
4 SERVINGS

3 whole-wheat pita pockets, each cut into 6 wedges with the top layer separated from the bottom

½ teaspoon garlic powder
½ teaspoon smoked paprika
¼ teaspoon coarse kosher salt
2 tablespoons olive oil

1. Preheat the oven to 400°F. Line two sheet pans with silicone baking mats or parchment paper.

2. Divide the pita wedges between the two sheet pans. Sprinkle ¼ teaspoon of garlic powder, ¼ teaspoon of paprika, ⅛ teaspoon of salt, and 1 tablespoon of oil over the pita on each sheet pan. Carefully toss the pita until coated with the oil and spices and arrange the chips on the pans, making sure they don't overlap.

3. Bake for 5 minutes. Using tongs, flip the chips over. Rotate the bottom pan to the top rack and vice versa and bake for another 2 minutes, or until the chips are crisp.

4. Serve at room temperature.

STORAGE TIP: Homemade pita chips will stay fresh for up to 4 days when stored in an airtight container at room temperature.

PER SERVING: Calories: 188; Total fat: 8g; Saturated fat: 1g; Sodium: 331g; Total carbohydrates: 27g; Sugar: 1g; Fiber: 3g; Protein: 5g; Calcium: 8mg

PREP TIME:
10 minutes

MAKES
2 SERVINGS

Hummus Toast with Cucumber and Feta

Avocado isn't the only ingredient that goes well on toast. Hummus toast is also a delicious snack or even a savory breakfast. Feel free to use a variety of veggies including sliced radish, tomato, red onion, baby spinach, and arugula. You can use store-bought hummus if you are short on time.

2 slices whole-wheat bread
¼ cup Lemony Parsley
  Hummus (page 44) or
  store-bought hummus
1 cup sliced English or
  Persian cucumber

2 tablespoons crumbled
  feta cheese
Pinch freshly ground
  black pepper
1 teaspoon olive oil

1. Toast the bread. Spread each slice with 2 tablespoons of hummus.

2. Top each slice of hummus toast with ½ cup of sliced cucumber, 1 tablespoon of feta, a pinch of pepper, and ½ teaspoon of oil.

3. Serve at room temperature.

INGREDIENT TIP: Just because the package of bread in the store says the words "wheat bread," it does not mean that the bread is made predominantly of whole grains. When shopping for whole-wheat bread, make sure the first ingredient on the ingredient list is actually "whole wheat."

PER SERVING: Calories: 188; Total fat: 8g; Saturated fat: 2g; Sodium: 307g; Total carbohydrates: 22g; Sugar: 3g; Fiber: 3g; Protein: 7g; Calcium: 122mg

Prosciutto-Wrapped Melon with Mint and Arugula

DAIRY-FREE
15-MINUTE
5-INGREDIENT
GLUTEN-FREE
NO-COOK
NUT-FREE

PREP TIME:
10 minutes

MAKES
4 SERVINGS

Melon wrapped with prosciutto is a classic Italian appetizer that typically consists of just those two ingredients. I added a little bit of greenery to freshen things up and give it a little bit of roughage. It's almost like having a tiny salad on top of each piece of cantaloupe.

4 slices prosciutto
20 fresh mint leaves
2 cups packed arugula

1¼ pounds cantaloupe, peeled, seeded, and cut into 20 (1-by-3-inch) slices, ¼ inch thick

1. Cut each slice of prosciutto into 5 long strips.

2. Place 1 mint leaf and 3 or 4 pieces of arugula on top of 1 cantaloupe slice. Wrap the prosciutto strip around the mint, arugula, and cantaloupe and secure with a toothpick, if desired. Repeat with the remaining ingredients.

3. Serve at room temperature.

VARIATION TIP: You can also try this recipe with honeydew instead of cantaloupe and fresh basil leaves in place of the mint.

PER SERVING: Calories: 68; Total fat: 2g; Saturated fat: 1g; Sodium: 328g; Total carbohydrates: 10g; Sugar: 9g; Fiber: 1g; Protein: 5g; Calcium: 21mg

Savory Yogurt Parfait with Cherry Tomatoes, Avocado, and Pine Nuts

Homemade yogurt parfaits are delicious and healthy snacks, but you may not always feel like a sweet option. You'll love this savory version if you're like me and crave savory snacks more often than sweet ones. To make this preparation extra quick, I chose ingredients that don't need to be cooked, but feel free to use a variety of cooked veggies, including roasted broccoli, butternut squash, or sautéed mushrooms.

1½ cups cherry tomatoes, quartered or halved

½ avocado, diced

1 tablespoon capers, drained and chopped

2 tablespoons pine nuts

3½ teaspoons olive oil, divided

1 teaspoon white wine vinegar

⅛ teaspoon coarse kosher salt

¼ teaspoon freshly ground black pepper

1½ cups low-fat (2 percent) plain Greek yogurt

1. In a medium bowl, mix together the tomatoes, avocado, capers, nuts, 2 teaspoons of oil, vinegar, salt, and pepper until combined. Taste, and add more salt or vinegar, if desired.

2. Spoon ½ cup of yogurt into each of three bowls and place ½ cup of the tomato mixture over each portion of yogurt. Drizzle ½ teaspoon oil over each serving.

3. Enjoy at room temperature.

COOKING TIP: If you feel like turning on the stove, toast the pine nuts in a dry pan, shaking the pan often, until golden, 2 to 3 minutes.

PER SERVING: Calories: 216; Total fat: 15g; Saturated fat: 2g; Sodium: 166g; Total carbohydrates: 10g; Sugar: 6g; Fiber: 3g; Protein: 13g; Calcium: 141mg

Endive Spears with Smoked Salmon, Goat Cheese, and Chives

15-MINUTE
5-INGREDIENT
GLUTEN-FREE
NO-COOK
NUT-FREE

PREP TIME:
10 minutes

SERVES 4

Avoid boring snacks by incorporating different types of textures to your appetizers. The crispy endive, creamy goat cheese, and salty smoked salmon in this recipe create an explosion of flavor with every bite. If you are on a reduced-sodium diet, try substituting the smoked salmon with plain roasted salmon, which is also very tasty.

4 ounces sliced, cold-smoked salmon

3 endive heads, 20 of the largest leaves pulled off

½ cup crumbled soft goat cheese

2 tablespoons chopped fresh chives

1. Divide the salmon equally among the endive leaves, placing it in the well of each spear.

2. Top the salmon with the goat cheese and sprinkle with the chives.

3. Serve at room temperature.

VARIATION TIP: If you're not a fan of bitter greens, swap the endive for butter lettuce to make more of a wrap-style snack. Also, if you don't have goat cheese, you can use crumbled feta or cubes of fresh mozzarella.

PER SERVING (5 SPEARS): Calories: 77; Total fat: 4g; Saturated fat: 2g; Sodium: 441g; Total carbohydrates: 1g; Sugar: 0g; Fiber: 1g; Protein: 3g; Calcium: 35mg

Caprese Salad with
Balsamic Glaze, *page 53*

Salads and Sides

PREP TIME:
15 minutes

**MAKES
6 SERVINGS**

Cannellini Bean Salad with Capers and Parsley

Simple bean-based salads make great side dishes to bring to picnics or barbecues because they are flavorful, hearty, and best when served at room temperature. Feel free to use your favorite type of beans, or even use a mixture.

2 (15-ounce) cans cannellini beans, drained and rinsed
½ cup chopped fresh parsley
⅓ cup finely chopped shallot
1 teaspoon finely chopped garlic
3 tablespoons capers, drained, rinsed, and chopped

2 tablespoons white wine vinegar
2 tablespoons olive oil
¼ teaspoon coarse kosher salt
Pinch freshly ground black pepper

In a large bowl, mix together the cannellini beans, parsley, shallot, garlic, capers, vinegar, oil, salt, and pepper. Taste and add more vinegar, if desired. Serve at room temperature.

INGREDIENT TIP: When using canned beans, always drain and rinse them before using. This simple process can actually lower the sodium content by around 40 percent.

PER SERVING: Calories: 120; Total fat: 5g; Saturated fat: 1g; Sodium: 220g; Total carbohydrates: 15g; Sugar: 1g; Fiber: 6g; Protein: 6g; Calcium: 429mg

Caprese Salad with Balsamic Glaze

15-MINUTE
GLUTEN-FREE
NO-COOK
NUT-FREE
VEGETARIAN

PREP TIME:
10 minutes

SERVES 4

Because there are so few ingredients in a caprese salad, its success depends on the quality of what you put in it. I recommend keeping a really nice extra-virgin olive oil on hand solely for the purpose of drizzling on top of finished dishes like this one. A peppery olive oil pairs very nicely with the flavors in a caprese salad. Although not traditional, I've added heart-healthy olives for extra texture and flavor. Be sure to buy fresh mozzarella instead of the low-moisture kind usually used for pizza.

1 pound vine-ripened or heirloom tomatoes, cut into ¼-inch-thick slices

6 ounces fresh mozzarella, cut into ⅛-inch-thick slices

25 fresh whole basil leaves

1 tablespoon peppery or grassy extra-virgin olive oil

1 tablespoon balsamic glaze

¼ teaspoon coarse kosher salt

Pinch freshly ground black pepper

20 small green pitted olives

1. Arrange alternate slices of tomato, mozzarella, and basil leaves on a large platter.

2. Evenly distribute any remaining basil leaves on top of the salad.

3. Drizzle the oil and balsamic glaze over the salad, sprinkle the salt and pepper, top with the olives, and serve immediately.

VARIATION TIP: To make your own balsamic glaze, pour ½ cup balsamic vinegar into a 3½-quart saucepan and bring to a boil. Lower the heat to medium and cook until the vinegar reduces and has a thick, syrupy consistency that coats the back of a spoon, about 6 minutes. Watch it like a hawk starting at 5 minutes to make sure it does not burn. The glaze will thicken as it cools.

PER SERVING: Calories: 194; Total fat: 14g; Saturated fat: 6g; Sodium: 413g; Total carbohydrates: 9g; Sugar: 5g; Fiber: 2g; Protein: 9g; Calcium: 195mg

Greek Salad

Greek salad is a classic item to keep in your recipe repertoire, and it's a classic Mediterranean mainstay for anyone following this kind of diet. Super fresh and flavorful, it's also a snap to make. To make this a main course salad, double the recipe and add a protein such as grilled shrimp, salmon, chicken, or baked tofu.

2 tablespoons red wine vinegar
1 teaspoon Dijon mustard
1 tablespoon water
¼ teaspoon dried oregano
⅛ teaspoon coarse kosher salt
3 tablespoons olive oil
4 cups chopped romaine lettuce

2 cups chopped English or Persian cucumber
1 cup halved cherry tomatoes (quartered if the tomatoes are large)
½ cup pitted Kalamata olives
½ cup crumbled feta cheese
⅓ cup coarsely chopped fresh mint leaves

1. In a small bowl, whisk together the vinegar, mustard, water, oregano, and salt. Whisk in the oil and set the dressing aside.

2. Place the lettuce, cucumber, tomatoes, olives, feta, and mint in a large bowl. Add the dressing and toss until combined.

3. Serve at room temperature.

COOKING TIP: Use a serrated paring knife to make cutting the tomatoes much easier.

PER SERVING: Calories: 210; Total fat: 19g; Saturated fat: 4g; Sodium: 380g; Total carbohydrates: 8g; Sugar: 3g; Fiber: 2g; Protein: 5g; Calcium: 116mg

Italian Chopped Salad with Rotisserie Chicken

GLUTEN-FREE
NO-COOK
NUT-FREE
30-MINUTE

PREP TIME:
20 minutes

MAKES
4 SERVINGS

I love chopped salads that contain many different flavors and textures. And when you just don't have the time or energy to cook, a store-bought rotisserie chicken can be a life-saver, especially on busy weekdays. If you need to watch the sodium, omit the pepperoncini and use Swiss instead of provolone.

¼ cup balsamic vinegar

2 tablespoons water

⅛ teaspoon coarse kosher salt

½ teaspoon honey

2 tablespoons olive oil

2 cups packed shredded, cooked rotisserie chicken

6 cups mixed greens

1 cup chopped English or Persian cucumber

1 cup cherry tomatoes, halved or quartered

1 cup canned low-sodium chickpeas, drained and rinsed

½ cup sliced pepperoncini, drained

1 cup coarsely chopped jarred roasted peppers

4 ounces sliced provolone cheese, cut into bite-size pieces

1. In a small bowl, whisk together the balsamic vinegar, water, salt, and honey. Add the oil and whisk until combined. Set the dressing aside.

2. In a large serving bowl, combine the chicken, mixed greens, cucumber, tomato, chickpeas, pepperoncini, peppers, and cheese. Add the dressing and toss until combined.

3. Serve at room temperature.

INGREDIENT TIP: When choosing jarred pepperoncini, be sure to look at the ingredient label and choose one that does not contain artificial colors.

PER SERVING: Calories: 371; Total fat: 19g; Saturated fat: 7g; Sodium: 779g; Total carbohydrates: 24g; Sugar: 10g; Fiber: 5g; Protein: 26g; Calcium: 265mg

PREP TIME:
10 minutes

COOK TIME:
30 minutes

SERVES 4

Roasted Carrots with Orange, Ginger, and Mint

Roasting brings out the natural sweetness in vegetables that you don't get from steaming or sautéing, thanks to the magic of caramelization. In addition to the fresh mint, a Mediterranean staple, try adding some toasted pistachios or walnuts after the carrots come out of the oven.

1 tablespoon olive oil
Zest and juice of 1 orange
2 teaspoons grated fresh ginger
1 teaspoon honey
¼ teaspoon coarse kosher salt

1¼ pounds carrots, peeled and cut into 1½-inch diagonal pieces
2 tablespoons coarsely chopped fresh mint

1. Preheat the oven to 400°F. Line a sheet pan with a silicone baking mat or parchment paper.

2. In a small bowl, mix together the oil, orange zest, 2 tablespoons of orange juice, ginger, honey, and salt.

3. Place the carrots on the prepared sheet pan, then pour the dressing over the carrots and toss until coated. Spread the carrots out as much as possible on the sheet pan.

4. Roast for 20 minutes, stir with a metal spatula, spread out the carrots again, and roast for another 10 minutes, or until the carrots are tender and browned around the edges.

5. Toss the carrots with the remaining 1 tablespoon of orange juice.

6. Transfer the carrots to a serving plate and toss with the mint. Serve warm or at room temperature.

COOKING TIP: Don't toss the carrots with the mint while they are still hot on the sheet pan. The mint will turn black.

PER SERVING: Calories: 73; Total fat: 4g; Saturated fat: 1g; Sodium: 174g; Total carbohydrates: 10g; Sugar: 5g; Fiber: 3g; Protein: 1g; Calcium: 34mg

Sautéed Zucchini and Shallots with Herbes de Provence

Sautéed zucchini is a quick, no-fuss, no-muss veggie side. Herbes de Provence, a fragrant dried herb blend from the South of France, is composed of thyme, basil, marjoram, fennel, rosemary, and lavender and smells heavenly. If you're a garlic lover, feel free to add 1 teaspoon of chopped garlic when you add the zucchini.

DAIRY-FREE
15-MINUTE
5-INGREDIENT
GLUTEN-FREE
NUT-FREE
ONE-POT
VEGAN

PREP TIME:
5 minutes

COOK TIME:
10 minutes

SERVES 4

1 tablespoon olive oil
½ cup thinly sliced shallots
1 pound zucchini, sliced

1 teaspoon dried herbes de Provence
¼ teaspoon coarse kosher salt
Pinch freshly ground pepper

1. Heat the oil in a 12-inch nonstick skillet over medium-high heat, until the oil is shimmering. Add the shallot and cook, stirring frequently, for 1 minute.

2. Add the zucchini, herbes de Provence, salt, and pepper and cook until the zucchini is crisp-tender, about 5 minutes.

3. Serve warm.

VARIATION TIP: If you can't find herbes de Provence, dried Italian herb seasoning can work in a pinch.

PER SERVING: Calories: 56; Total fat: 4g; Saturated fat: 1g; Sodium: 125g; Total carbohydrates: 5g; Sugar: 3g; Fiber: 2g; Protein: 2g; Calcium: 25mg

PREP TIME:
5 minutes

COOK TIME:
10 minutes

SERVES 4

Sautéed Mushrooms and Sugar Snap Peas with Tarragon

Cremini mushrooms are actually baby portobello mushrooms that are marketed as baby bellas. I like them because they have a slightly meatier flavor than standard button mushrooms. Mushrooms are nutritional superstars because they are one of the few foods that naturally contain vitamin D. The Mediterranean diet uses mushrooms extensively, and this recipe really showcases them. I buy pre-sliced mushrooms to speed up prep.

1 tablespoon olive oil
1 pound sliced baby bella mushrooms
8 ounces sugar snap peas, trimmed
1 teaspoon chopped garlic

2 teaspoons chopped fresh tarragon
¼ teaspoon coarse kosher salt
Pinch freshly ground black pepper
1 teaspoon lemon juice

1. Heat the oil a 12-inch nonstick skillet over medium-high heat until the oil is shimmering. Add the mushrooms and cook, without stirring, for 6 minutes.

2. Add the snap peas and garlic, stir, and continue cooking, until the snap peas are crisp-tender, 3 to 4 minutes.

3. Add the tarragon, salt, pepper, and lemon juice and stir until combined.

4. Serve warm.

COOKING TIP: Resist the urge to stir the mushrooms right away. By allowing them to cook without disturbing them for at least a few minutes, you'll get more browning, which means more flavor. Also, salt the mushrooms toward the end of cooking. Salting them at the beginning draws out water, which means you will end up steaming them.

PER SERVING: Calories: 73; Total fat: 4g; Saturated fat: 1g; Sodium: 122g; Total carbohydrates: 9g; Sugar: 4g; Fiber: 4g; Protein: 3g; Calcium: 30mg

Lebanese-Inspired Spiced Potatoes

DAIRY-FREE
GLUTEN-FREE
NUT-FREE
30-MINUTE
VEGAN

These potatoes have a little kick to them from the red chili flakes. If you don't like spicy foods, simply cut the amount of chili flakes in half. Tossing the potatoes with cilantro after cooking adds a bright, fresh taste, which complements the earthy spices.

PREP TIME:
5 minutes

COOK TIME:
20 minutes

SERVES 4

1 tablespoon plus 2 teaspoons olive oil
1 teaspoon ground coriander
½ teaspoon ground cumin
½ teaspoon ground turmeric
¼ teaspoon red chili flakes
1 teaspoon garlic powder
¼ teaspoon coarse kosher salt
⅛ teaspoon freshly ground black pepper
1¼ pounds red potatoes, cut into 1-inch pieces
¼ cup chopped fresh cilantro

1. Preheat the oven to 450°F. Line a sheet pan with a silicone baking mat or parchment paper.

2. In a small bowl, mix together the oil, coriander, cumin, turmeric, chili flakes, garlic powder, salt, and pepper.

3. Place the potatoes on the prepared sheet pan and spoon the spice paste over them. Using your hands, toss the potatoes until the spice mixture is evenly distributed over the potatoes.

4. Roast for 20 minutes, or until the potatoes are crispy.

5. Add the cilantro and toss until evenly distributed. Serve warm.

INGREDIENT TIP: The main active ingredient in turmeric is curcumin, which has powerful anti-inflammatory properties. It is even more powerful when combined with black pepper.

PER SERVING: Calories: 150; Total fat: 6g; Saturated fat: 1g; Sodium: 134g; Total carbohydrates: 22g; Sugar: 2g; Fiber: 2g; Protein: 3g; Calcium: 15mg

PREP TIME:
5 minutes

COOK TIME:
35 minutes

SERVES 4

Farro Pilaf

Farro is a hearty strain of wheat often referred to as an "ancient grain." Although farro is extremely popular in Italian cuisine, it actually originated in the Fertile Crescent in the Middle East, which includes parts of modern-day countries such as Syria and Turkey. I hate grating carrots because I always cut myself on the grater! I often buy pre-shredded carrots at the store to use in cold dishes like slaws and salads or hot dishes such as tomato sauce for pasta, soups, and pilafs. It's a great way to sneak some extra veggies into meals.

2 teaspoons olive oil
1 cup chopped red onion
1 teaspoon chopped garlic
½ cup shredded carrots
¾ cup farro

½ cup white wine
1¾ cups water
½ teaspoon coarse kosher salt

1. Heat the oil in a medium saucepan over medium-high heat until the oil is shimmering. Add the red onion, garlic, and carrots and cook, stirring occasionally, for 3 minutes.

2. Add the farro, stir, and cook for 1 minute. Add the white wine and cook for 1 minute more.

3. Add the water and salt, stir, raise the heat to high, and bring to a boil. Lower the heat to low, cover, and simmer until the farro is tender yet still has a little "bite," about 30 minutes. Serve warm.

PER SERVING: Calories: 220; Total fat: 3g; Saturated fat: 0g; Sodium: 257g; Total carbohydrates: 38g; Sugar: 6g; Fiber: 6g; Protein: 8g; Calcium: 26mg

Steamed Couscous with Golden Raisins and Pistachios

DAIRY-FREE
5-INGREDIENT
ONE-POT
30-MINUTE
VEGAN

PREP TIME:
10 minutes

COOK TIME:
10 minutes

SERVES 4

Did you know that couscous is actually pasta? Popular in North Africa, couscous is often served with hearty stews. Because the little spheres are so small, couscous cooks incredibly fast, which makes it great for weeknight cooking. Purchase the whole-wheat version if your supermarket carries it, for added health benefits.

2 teaspoons olive oil

½ cup finely chopped red onion

¾ cup water

¼ teaspoon coarse kosher salt

¾ cup whole-wheat couscous

½ cup chopped fresh parsley

⅓ cup shelled pistachios

⅓ cup golden raisins

1. Heat the oil in a medium saucepan over medium heat until the oil is shimmering. Add the red onion and cook, stirring frequently, for 2 minutes.

2. Add the water and salt and bring to a boil. Add the couscous, cover, and turn off the heat. Leave couscous covered until tender, about 5 minutes.

3. Add the parsley, pistachios, and raisins and stir until combined and the couscous is fluffy.

4. Serve warm.

VARIATION TIP: Chopped dates or dried apricots can be used in place of golden raisins.

PER SERVING: Calories: 190; Total fat: 8g; Saturated fat: 1g; Sodium: 132g; Total carbohydrates: 27g; Sugar: 8g; Fiber: 3g; Protein: 5g; Calcium: 38mg

PREP TIME:
10 minutes

COOK TIME:
25 minutes

SERVES 4

Simple Oven-Baked Sweet Potato Fries

One of the secrets to achieving crisp, browned oven-baked fries is to spread out the pieces of potato on the sheet pan as much as possible. In fact, I call for two sheet pans here to give the sweet potatoes enough space to "breathe" so they will be as crunchy as possible and not end up steamed and soggy. The coating of cornstarch is an additional aid to make the sweet potato crispier.

1½ pounds sweet potatoes, peeled and cut into ¼-inch-thick sticks
2 teaspoons cornstarch, divided

½ teaspoon coarse kosher salt, divided
4 teaspoons olive oil, divided
½ teaspoon garlic powder

1. Preheat the oven to 425°F. Line two sheet pans with silicone baking mats or parchment paper.

2. Spread out the sweet potatoes evenly between both sheet pans. Sprinkle 1 teaspoon of cornstarch and ¼ teaspoon of salt over the potatoes in each pan. Toss until combined, making sure there aren't any clumps of cornstarch remaining.

3. Pour 2 teaspoons of oil over each sheet pan of fries and toss until coated, making sure to spread them out in a single layer. Place one pan on the top rack and the other pan on the bottom rack. Bake for 15 minutes.

4. Using a metal spatula, flip the fries. Rotate the bottom pan to the top rack and vice versa. Bake for another 10 minutes. If the fries don't look crispy, bake them for 2 to 5 minutes more, watching very closely to make sure they don't burn.

5. Sprinkle the garlic powder over the fries and toss until evenly coated.

6. Serve hot.

COOKING TIP: Try to cut the sweet potatoes (or any vegetables you intend to roast) into uniform sizes to ensure even cooking.

PER SERVING: Calories: 103; Total fat: 5g; Saturated fat: 1g; Sodium: 392g; Total carbohydrates: 14g; Sugar: 4g; Fiber: 2g; Protein: 1g; Calcium: 24mg

**Roasted Tomato and
Red Pepper Soup,** *page 68*

Soups and Sandwiches

PREP TIME:
10 minutes

COOK TIME:
30 minutes

SERVES 6

Black-Eyed Pea, Chard, and Rice Soup with Dill and Lemon

Black-eyed peas, also known as cowpeas, are definitely an underrated legume, but they are so delicious in soups, stews, salads, and sides. They are used often in Greek cuisine. Instant brown rice works well for this soup because it has a firm texture, yet cooks quickly. Don't worry: Even though the rice is "instant," it's still considered a whole grain.

1 tablespoon olive oil
1 bunch scallions, white and green parts, chopped
2 teaspoons chopped garlic
1 bunch chard, stems and leaves coarsely chopped (keep stems and leaves separate)
2 tablespoons tomato paste

5 cups water
⅔ cup instant brown rice
1 (15.5-ounce) can black-eyed peas, drained and rinsed
¾ teaspoon coarse kosher salt
1 tablespoon lemon juice
¼ cup chopped fresh dill

1. Heat the oil in a large pot over medium-high heat until the oil is shimmering. Add the scallions, garlic, and chard stems and cook for 4 minutes. Add the tomato paste and cook, stirring constantly, for 1 minute. Add the chard leaves and cook, stirring occasionally, for another 5 minutes.

2. Add the water, rice, and black-eyed peas, stir, increase the heat to high, and bring to a boil. Lower the heat to low and simmer, stirring often, until the vegetables are tender, about 20 minutes.

3. Add the salt, lemon juice, and dill and stir until combined. Taste, and adjust the seasoning, if desired.

4. Serve hot.

STORAGE TIP: This soup can be stored in an airtight container and frozen for up to 6 months.

PER SERVING: Calories: 133; Total fat: 3g; Saturated fat: 0g; Sodium: 423g; Total carbohydrates: 22g; Sugar: 3g; Fiber: 4g; Protein: 5g; Calcium: 71mg

Moroccan-Spiced Lentil and Vegetable Soup

BIG-BATCH
DAIRY-FREE
NUT-FREE
ONE-POT
VEGAN

PREP TIME:
10 minutes

COOK TIME:
30 minutes

SERVES 6

Lentils are a wonderful source of plant-based protein, containing 9 grams per ½-cup serving. Plus, each serving of this soup has 8 grams of fiber. This is a great soup to meal prep at the beginning of the week because the flavors continue to develop as it sits in the refrigerator.

1 tablespoon olive oil

1 small onion, chopped

2 medium carrots, chopped

1 large celery stalk, chopped

1 teaspoon chopped garlic

1 teaspoon ground cumin

1½ teaspoons ground coriander

1 teaspoon ground turmeric

1 cup dried brown lentils

1 (14.5-ounce) can no-salt-added diced tomatoes

6 cups water

1 teaspoon coarse kosher salt

¼ cup chopped fresh cilantro

1 teaspoon lemon juice

1. Heat the oil in a large pot over medium-high heat until the oil is shimmering. Add the onion, carrot, celery, and garlic and cook until the onions start to brown, about 8 minutes. Add the cumin, coriander, and turmeric and cook, stirring frequently, for another 2 minutes.

2. Add the lentils, tomatoes, and water and bring to a boil. Lower the heat to low and simmer for 30 minutes. Add the salt, cilantro, and lemon juice and stir until combined.

3. Taste, and adjust the seasoning, if desired. Serve hot.

STORAGE TIP: The soup can be stored in an airtight container and frozen for up to 3 months.

PER SERVING: Calories: 149; Total fat: 3g; Saturated fat: 0g; Sodium: 362g; Total carbohydrates: 24g; Sugar: 6g; Fiber: 8g; Protein: 8g; Calcium: 63mg

PREP TIME:
10 minutes,
plus
10 minutes
to cool

COOK TIME:
1 hour

SERVES 4

Roasted Tomato and Red Pepper Soup

This isn't your average tomato soup in a can. It has such a luscious, creamy texture that you might think it includes dairy, but it doesn't! The sweet roasted tomatoes and peppers meld with the smokiness of the paprika, the acidity of the vinegar, and the slight oniony bite of the chives. This is the ultimate soup to pair with a grilled cheese sandwich. To elevate the presentation, mix in a couple of teaspoons of fresh thyme leaves and add a thyme sprig to garnish.

3 pounds Roma tomatoes, halved

1 pound red bell peppers, stemmed, seeded, and halved

2 tablespoons olive oil, plus 1 teaspoon

1 teaspoon smoked paprika

1 tablespoon red wine vinegar

½ teaspoon coarse kosher salt

½ cup water

4 teaspoons minced fresh chives

1. Preheat the oven to 400°F. Line a sheet pan with a silicone baking mat or parchment paper. If your sheet pan doesn't have a rim, use a baking dish instead because juices will accumulate.

2. Place the tomatoes and red peppers on the pan, pour 2 tablespoons of oil over them, and toss until coated. Spread the vegetables into one layer and roast for 50 minutes to 1 hour, or until tender. Let cool on the sheet pan for 10 minutes.

3. Carefully transfer the veggies to a blender. Add the smoked paprika, vinegar, salt, water, and any pan juices to the blender and blend until smooth.

4. Divide the soup among four bowls. Sprinkle each serving with 1 teaspoon of chives and drizzle with ¼ teaspoon of the remaining oil.

5. Serve hot.

COOKING TIP: Be very careful when opening the lid of the blender when pureeing hot liquids. Cover the lid with a kitchen towel before you turn on the blender and when removing the lid, be sure to open it away from you.

PER SERVING: Calories: 129; Total fat: 9g; Saturated fat: 1g; Sodium: 266g; Total carbohydrates: 13g; Sugar: 8g; Fiber: 3g; Protein: 3g; Calcium: 32mg

PREP TIME:
15 minutes

**COOK
TIME:** 1 hour
10 minutes

SERVES 4

Mediterranean Vegetable Soup

If you have veggies that are just about past their prime, don't throw them out—make soup! Veggie soup is one of those great clean-out-the-refrigerator kind of meals, so feel free to substitute these veggies with others that you have on hand. I topped this soup with a sprinkle of Parmesan cheese, but you can also swirl a dollop of pesto into each bowl. Either way, it makes a wonderful Italian meal.

1 tablespoon olive oil
½ medium onion, chopped
1 leek, white part only, thinly sliced
2 teaspoons chopped garlic
½ large fennel bulb, thinly sliced
2 medium carrots, peeled and cut into ½-inch pieces
1 cup dry white wine
1½ teaspoons herbes de Provence

2 medium red potatoes, cut into ½-inch pieces
1 medium zucchini, cut into ½-inch slices
2 cups chopped green cabbage
5 cups water
1 teaspoon coarse kosher salt
4 tablespoons grated Parmesan cheese

1. Heat the oil in a large pot over medium heat until the oil is shimmering. Add the onion, leek, garlic, fennel, and carrot, and cook, stirring occasionally, for 8 minutes.

2. Add the wine, stir, and cook for 2 minutes. Add the herbes de Provence, potatoes, zucchini, cabbage, and water, increase the heat to high, and bring to a boil. Lower the heat to low and simmer for 1 hour.

3. Divide the soup among four bowls, sprinkle 1 tablespoon Parmesan over each serving, and serve hot.

INGREDIENT TIP: When cooking with white wine, you want a dry, crisp wine, high in acidity. Try sauvignon blanc, Pinot Grigio, Pinot Gris, or an unoaked Chardonnay.

PER SERVING: Calories: 186; Total fat: 5g; Saturated fat: 2g; Sodium: 581g; Total carbohydrates: 21g; Sugar: 5g; Fiber: 4g; Protein: 5g; Calcium: 136mg

Fisherman's Stew

The beauty of this stew is that you can use basically whatever type of seafood you want. I've called for shrimp and white fish here, though clams, mussels, bay scallops, or crab would also work well. Some supermarkets even sell bags of mixed seafood specifically for making seafood stews like this one. Serve with a slice of crusty bread so diners can soak up the very flavorful broth. Cut the amount of chili flakes in half if you prefer less heat.

DAIRY-FREE
GLUTEN-FREE
NUT-FREE
ONE-POT

PREP TIME:
10 minutes

COOK TIME:
50 minutes

SERVES 4

2 tablespoons olive oil
1 cup chopped onion
1 cup chopped fennel
2 teaspoons chopped garlic
¼ teaspoon red chili flakes
1 (28-ounce) can no-salt-added diced tomatoes
1 cup white wine
2 cups clam juice

¾ pound any white fish, such as cod, snapper, or tilapia
1 pound peeled and deveined large shrimp
½ teaspoon coarse kosher salt
Pinch freshly ground black pepper
3 tablespoons chopped fresh basil

1. Heat the oil in a large pot over medium heat until the oil is shimmering. Add the onion, fennel, garlic, and chili flakes and cook, stirring occasionally, for 8 minutes.

2. Add the tomatoes, wine, and clam juice, raise the heat to high, and bring to a boil. Lower the heat to low and simmer for 30 minutes.

3. Add the fish and shrimp to the pot, cover, and continue to cook, until the seafood is cooked, about 10 minutes.

4. Add the salt and pepper and stir until combined. Taste, and adjust the seasoning, if desired.

5. Ladle the stew into bowls and garnish each serving with the basil.

VARIATION TIP: To make this dish even heartier, add cooked pasta to each bowl just before serving.

PER SERVING: Calories: 328; Total fat: 10g; Saturated fat: 2g; Sodium: 726g; Total carbohydrates: 13g; Sugar: 7g; Fiber: 5g; Protein: 40g; Calcium: 157mg

PREP TIME:
10 minutes

COOK TIME:
20 minutes

SERVES 4

Veggie Panini with Pesto

Ciabatta rolls are the perfect size for a satisfying sandwich. If your store doesn't carry them, you can purchase a whole loaf and cut it into 3½-by-3½-inch pieces. Be sure to cut your eggplant and zucchini into ¼-inch-thick slices so they cook quickly and evenly. Roasted tomatoes or sun-dried tomatoes would also be a tasty addition.

6 ounces eggplant, cut into 4 (¼-inch-thick) slices

1 large zucchini, halved lengthwise, each half cut into 8 (¼-inch-thick) slices

1 tablespoon olive oil, plus 1 teaspoon

½ teaspoon dried oregano

⅛ teaspoon red chili flakes

½ cup pesto

4 (3-by-4-inch) slices jarred roasted red pepper

1½ cups packed baby spinach

4 (4-ounce) ciabatta rolls, split

1. Preheat the oven to 425°F. Line a sheet pan with a silicone baking mat or parchment paper.

2. Place the eggplant and zucchini in one layer on the sheet pan. Drizzle with 1 tablespoon of oil and sprinkle with oregano and chili flakes. Toss until they are evenly coated. Spread the slices out into one layer again and roast for 7 minutes. Flip the slices over and roast for an additional 5 to 7 minutes, or until the veggies are tender.

3. Spread 1 tablespoon of pesto on the top and bottom pieces of the bread. Build the sandwiches by layering 1 piece of pepper, 2 slices of zucchini, 1 slice of eggplant, and the spinach.

4. Heat the remaining 1 teaspoon of oil in a 12-inch skillet over medium heat until the oil is hot. Place the sandwiches in the pan, press them down with a heavy skillet, such as cast iron, and continue to press down, until toasted, about 1 minute, on each side.

5. Cut the sandwiches in half and serve warm.

COOKING TIP: Most bread contains a fair amount of salt, which is used for taste and for creating the structure of the bread. If you follow a lower-sodium diet, use low-sodium wheat bread from brands such as Angelic Bakehouse or Food for Life Ezekiel bread. If you use an alternate bread like this, you may need to press the sandwich for a little less time.

PER SERVING: Calories: 413; Total fat: 19g; Saturated fat: 3g; Sodium: 864g; Total carbohydrates: 51g; Sugar: 4g; Fiber: 4g; Protein: 10g; Calcium: 86mg

Chickpea Salad Pita Sandwich

If you're looking for an easy and filling meatless sandwich option, rich with fiber and the sunny antioxidants of the Mediterranean, look no further. I always use canned chickpeas for convenience and try to choose lower-sodium options. Be sure to read the nutrition label on the can. I find that organic options often contain less sodium than some of the brands that are marketed as "reduced sodium" or "low sodium." Aim for no more than 130 milligrams of sodium per ½-cup serving. Draining and rinsing the chickpeas further reduces that amount by about 40 percent.

1 (15-ounce) can low-sodium chickpeas, drained and rinsed
½ cup finely chopped celery
1 teaspoon Dijon mustard
2 teaspoons lemon juice
⅓ cup low-fat (2 percent) plain Greek yogurt

¼ cup chopped chives
¼ cup chopped parsley
2 teaspoons olive oil
¼ teaspoon coarse kosher salt
2 whole-wheat pita pockets, each cut in half
4 slices tomato

1. In a large bowl, mash the chickpeas with a potato masher until they are somewhat smooth but still chunky.

2. Add the celery, mustard, lemon juice, yogurt, chives, parsley, oil, and salt and mix until combined.

3. Place ½ cup of the chickpea mixture and 1 tomato slice into each pita pocket half.

4. Enjoy at room temperature.

PER SERVING: Calories: 184; Total fat: 4g; Saturated fat: 0g; Sodium: 385g; Total carbohydrates: 30g; Sugar: 4g; Fiber: 6g; Protein: 8g; Calcium: 59mg

White Bean, Spinach, and Sun-Dried Tomato Quesadilla

NUT-FREE
30-MINUTE
VEGETARIAN

PREP TIME:
15 minutes

COOK TIME:
15 minutes

SERVES 4

Quesadillas are one of the easiest and quickest meals around, but they usually aren't very healthy. The good news is that by using less cheese, adding beans as a plant-based protein spread, and incorporating antioxidant-rich veggies, you can cook up a better-for-you quesadilla.

1 (15-ounce) can low-sodium white beans, drained and rinsed

1 teaspoon chopped garlic

2 teaspoons lemon juice

1 teaspoon olive oil

¼ teaspoon coarse kosher salt

½ teaspoon dried Italian herb seasoning

1 cup frozen spinach, thawed and squeezed to remove excess water

¾ cup shredded part-skim mozzarella cheese

⅓ cup sliced sun-dried tomatoes in olive oil, drained

⅓ cup thinly sliced red onion

4 whole-wheat tortillas

1. In a large bowl, combine the beans, garlic, lemon juice, oil, salt, and Italian seasoning. Using a potato masher, mash the beans until mostly smooth.

2. In a medium bowl, mix together the spinach, cheese, tomatoes, and onion.

3. Place 1 tortilla on a clean work surface. Spread ¼ cup of the bean mixture onto half of the tortilla. Top with ½ cup of the spinach mixture. Fold the empty half of the tortilla over the filled half. Repeat with the other three tortillas.

4. Heat a 12-inch nonstick skillet over medium heat. When hot, add 2 of the quesadillas and cook until the tortillas are slightly crisp and the cheese is melted, 2 to 3 minutes on each side. Repeat with the remaining 2 quesadillas.

5. Cut each quesadilla into 3 pieces and serve warm.

PER SERVING: Calories: 268; Total fat: 10g; Saturated fat: 5g; Sodium: 470g; Total carbohydrates: 32g; Sugar: 2g; Fiber: 8g; Protein: 13g; Calcium: 513mg

Herbed Tuna, Cucumber, and Arugula Lavash Wrap

Canned tuna is a convenient and cost-effective way to include seafood in your diet. I prefer the pouches to the cans because there is less water and less mess, and you're less likely to cut yourself on the can, which I always seem to do. I used reduced-sodium tuna for this recipe, but to cut the sodium even more, purchase a no-salt-added tuna.

3 (2.6-ounce) pouches reduced-sodium light tuna in water, drained
¼ cup chopped fresh dill
3 tablespoons finely chopped red onion
1 tablespoon lemon juice
2 teaspoons olive oil
¼ teaspoon coarse kosher salt
Pinch freshly ground black pepper

4 (9-by-6-inch) pieces fresh lavash, preferably whole-wheat
½ cup Lemony Parsley Hummus (page 44) or store-bought hummus
1 cup sliced English or Persian cucumber
1½ cups packed arugula
8 thin slices tomato

1. In a medium bowl, mix together the tuna, dill, onion, lemon juice, oil, salt, and pepper.

2. Place 1 piece of lavash on a clean work surface with the short edge closest to you. Spread 2 tablespoons of hummus on the half of the lavash closest to you. Top with ¼ cup of cucumber, ⅓ cup of arugula, 2 slices of tomato, and ⅓ cup of the tuna mixture.

3. Roll the lavash away from you until the wrap is fully rolled and looks like a burrito. Repeat with the other pieces of lavash and filling.

4. Serve at room temperature.

PER SERVING: Calories: 255; Total fat: 6g; Saturated fat: 1g; Sodium: 565g; Total carbohydrates: 33g; Sugar: 2g; Fiber: 3g; Protein: 19g; Calcium: 43mg

Mediterranean Lamb Burger

Lamb is a popular meat served around the Mediterranean, especially in Greece, Turkey, France, and Algeria. When I make any type of burger, I always blend the meat with some sort of veggie, such as chopped spinach, mushrooms, or zucchini, for extra nutrients and to stretch the meat further. For condiments, I recommend serving this with arugula, jarred roasted red peppers, and a yogurt-based sauce such as Tzatziki Sauce (page 170).

PREP TIME:
10 minutes

COOK TIME:
15 minutes

SERVES 6

6 ounces zucchini, grated
1 pound ground lamb
1 egg
½ cup chopped fresh cilantro
¼ cup panko bread crumbs
1½ teaspoons ground cumin
2 teaspoons paprika
2 teaspoons onion powder

2 teaspoons garlic powder
½ teaspoon coarse kosher salt
Optional toppings:
  whole-wheat buns, leafy
  greens, roasted red
  peppers, sliced tomato,
  tzatziki sauce

1. Place the zucchini in a clean kitchen towel and squeeze out as much water as possible.

2. In a large bowl, combine the lamb, egg, cilantro, bread crumbs, cumin, paprika, onion powder, garlic powder, and salt and, using your hands, mix together until well blended.

3. Preheat a charcoal or gas grill to medium heat.

4. Grill the patties until the middle is no longer pink, 6 to 7 minutes on each side. If you don't have a grill, cook the patties in a dry skillet over medium heat for 6 to 7 minutes per side.

5. Serve warm with a bun and any desired toppings (if using).

STORAGE TIP: Line a plate with plastic wrap or parchment paper, place uncooked patties on the plate in a single layer, and freeze. When the patties are frozen, place them in an airtight container or zip-top plastic bag and return to the freezer for up to 4 months.

PER SERVING: Calories: 189; Total fat: 11g; Saturated fat: 5g; Sodium: 251g; Total carbohydrates: 6g; Sugar: 1g; Fiber: 1g; Protein: 15g; Calcium: 36mg

Stuffed Grape Leaves with Bulgur,
Lentils, and Dill, *page 104*

Vegetarian and Vegan

PREP TIME:
15 minutes

COOK TIME:
6 hours

SERVES 6

Slow Cooker–Braised Chard, Eggplant, and Butter Beans

Chard is such an under-appreciated leafy green vegetable. It's the perfect no-waste veggie because you can eat both the leaves and the stems. If you're not familiar with butter beans, you may see them labeled as lima beans, depending on the brand. I like to serve this dish with simple steamed bulgur or couscous.

2 cups chopped onion

2 teaspoons chopped garlic

2 tablespoons oil

1 pound eggplant, cut into 1-inch cubes

1 large bunch chard, stems and leaves roughly chopped

2 medium tomatoes, chopped

3 tablespoons tomato paste dissolved in ¾ cup hot water

2 teaspoons ground coriander

2 teaspoons dried oregano

2 (15.5-ounce) cans butter (or lima) beans, drained and rinsed

1 teaspoon kosher salt

2 teaspoons lemon juice

1. Place the onion, garlic, oil, eggplant, chard, tomatoes, tomato paste, coriander, oregano, and butter beans into a slow cooker.

2. Set the slow cooker low and cook for 6 hours.

3. Add the salt and 1 teaspoon of lemon juice and stir until combined. Taste, and add the remaining 1 teaspoon of lemon juice, if desired.

4. Serve hot.

STORAGE TIP: This dish freezes very well. For the best quality, store in an airtight container and freeze for up to 6 months.

PER SERVING: Calories: 174; Total fat: 5g; Saturated fat: 1g; Sodium: 504g; Total carbohydrates: 29g; Sugar: 8g; Fiber: 8g; Protein: 7g; Calcium: 91mg

Baked Falafel Patties

Falafel is a very popular dish in countries such as Israel and Egypt, and they're traditionally fried. I lightened up the recipe by baking them in the oven instead. Serve the falafels on their own, on top of a salad, or in a pita pocket. They are delicious with Garlic Tahini Sauce (page 169) or Shallot Yogurt (page 134).

BIG-BATCH
DAIRY-FREE
GLUTEN-FREE
NUT-FREE
VEGAN

PREP TIME:
15 minutes,
plus overnight
to soak

COOK TIME:
30 minutes

SERVES 6

1 cup dried chickpeas, soaked in water for at least 8 hours
2 cups chopped fresh parsley
2 teaspoons ground cumin
2 teaspoons ground coriander
⅛ teaspoon cayenne pepper
3 garlic cloves
½ medium white onion, very coarsely chopped
2 tablespoons lemon juice
3 tablespoons olive oil, divided
¾ teaspoon coarse kosher salt
1½ teaspoons baking powder

1. Preheat the oven to 400°F. Line a sheet pan with a silicone baking mat or parchment paper.

2. Combine the chickpeas, parsley, cumin, coriander, cayenne, garlic, onion, lemon juice, 1 tablespoon of oil, and salt in the bowl of a food processor. Process until mostly smooth, scraping down the sides of the bowl when necessary.

3. Transfer the mixture to a large bowl, add the baking powder, and stir until combined.

4. Spread the remaining 2 tablespoons of oil over the sheet pan. Spoon 12 equal-size scoops of the chickpea mixture onto the pan and form them into 2-inch patties.

5. Bake for 15 minutes. Flip the falafel and bake for another 30 minutes.

6. Serve immediately.

STORAGE TIP: Place the patties on a parchment-lined sheet pan and freeze. Once the falafels are frozen, transfer them to an airtight container or zip-top plastic bag and freeze for up to 6 months.

PER SERVING: Calories: 184; Total fat: 9g; Saturated fat: 1g; Sodium: 373g; Total carbohydrates: 22g; Sugar: 5g; Fiber: 6g; Protein: 6g; Calcium: 124mg

PREP TIME:
10 minutes

COOK TIME:
20 minutes

SERVES 4

Kale and Black Bean Stuffed Sweet Potatoes with Creamy Avocado Sauce

Sweet potatoes provide a hearty and nutritious base for a variety of tasty toppings. You can even top them with yogurt and honey and serve them for a simple breakfast. Sweet potatoes get their beautiful orange color from beta-carotene, which is an antioxidant that gets converted into vision-supporting vitamin A in our bodies.

4 red garnet sweet potatoes, about 5-by-2-inches each
3 tablespoons olive oil, divided
1 cup chopped red onion
1 medium bunch lacinato or curly kale, ribs removed, leaves roughly chopped
1 (15.5-ounce) can low-sodium black beans, drained and rinsed

1 tablespoon nutritional yeast
¾ teaspoon coarse kosher salt, divided
1 small avocado, pitted and peeled
½ teaspoon chopped garlic
1 cup packed chopped fresh parsley
½ cup chopped fresh mint
3 tablespoons lemon juice
½ cup water

1. Prick the sweet potatoes in multiple places with a fork. Place them on a microwave-safe plate and microwave on high for 10 minutes, or until the sweet potatoes are tender.

2. Heat 1 tablespoon of oil in a 12-inch sauté pan over medium-high heat until the oil is shimmering. Add the onion and cook, stirring often, for 2 minutes. Add the kale, black beans, nutritional yeast, and ¼ teaspoon of salt and cook, stirring often, for 8 minutes.

3. While the veggies are cooking, place the avocado, garlic, parsley, mint, lemon juice, water, the remaining 2 tablespoons of oil, and the remaining ½ teaspoon of salt in a blender and blend until smooth. Set aside.

4. When the potatoes are cool enough to handle, cut each potato down the middle lengthwise to open up the potato, making sure not to cut it all the way through. Using a fork, fluff the flesh until loosened. Spoon ½ cup of the veggie mixture on top of each potato and drizzle with ¼ cup of avocado sauce.

5. Serve warm.

COOKING TIP: To cook the sweet potatoes in the oven instead of a microwave, prick the potatoes all over with a fork and bake in a 425°F oven for 40 to 45 minutes, until tender. You'll get more delicious caramelization of the natural sugars with this method.

PER SERVING: Calories: 343; Total fat: 17g; Saturated fat: 2g; Sodium: 462g; Total carbohydrates: 44g; Sugar: 10g; Fiber: 11g; Protein: 9g; Calcium: 138mg

Stuffed Bell Peppers with Quinoa, Kidney Beans, and Mozzarella

With stuffed peppers, you basically have a whole meal—veggies, whole grains, beans, and cheese—inside a pepper. Plus, stuffed peppers freeze very well so if you keep some frozen, you'll have a balanced meal whenever you like. Marinated artichokes and canned ones don't have a huge difference in sodium content, so I chose the product with the most flavor—marinated.

¾ cup dry quinoa

1½ cups water

2 teaspoons chopped garlic

1 (12-ounce) jar marinated artichoke hearts, drained

1 (15-ounce) can low-sodium kidney beans, drained and rinsed

1 bunch scallions, white and green parts, chopped

2 tablespoons balsamic vinegar

½ cup chopped fresh basil

½ teaspoon coarse kosher salt

3 tablespoons olive oil, divided

6 medium red bell peppers

1 cup shredded mozzarella cheese

1. Preheat the oven to 400°F. Line a sheet pan with a silicone baking mat or parchment paper. If the sheet pan doesn't have a rim, use a baking dish instead.

2. Combine the quinoa and water in a saucepan and bring to a boil over high heat. Cover, lower the heat to low, and simmer for 15 minutes.

3. While the quinoa is cooking, in a large bowl, mix together the garlic, artichokes, beans, scallions, balsamic vinegar, basil, salt, and 1 tablespoon of oil.

4. Stand the peppers upright and cut them in half from stem to bottom. Remove the stems, seeds, and membranes.

5. Pour the remaining 2 tablespoons of oil onto the prepared sheet pan. Roll the peppers in the oil, using your hands to coat the inside and outside of the peppers. Arrange the peppers, open-side up, on the pan.

6. Add the quinoa to the artichoke mixture and mix until combined. Spoon ½ cup of the quinoa mixture into each pepper half. Cover the pan with aluminum foil and bake for 35 minutes, or until the peppers are tender.

7. Remove the foil and sprinkle the cheese over the stuffed peppers. Continue baking for another 10 minutes until the cheese is melted and slightly browned.

STORAGE TIP: Cooked stuffed peppers may be frozen for up to 6 months. If you are freezing the peppers, cook them without the cheese. Place the peppers in an airtight container. When ready to cook, bake in a 350°F oven for 20 minutes. Add the cheese and cook for another 5 to 10 minutes, until the cheese is melted and browned.

PER SERVING: Calories: 289; Total fat: 10g; Saturated fat: 1g; Sodium: 473g; Total carbohydrates: 39g; Sugar: 10g; Fiber: 8g; Protein: 15g; Calcium: 243mg

GLUTEN-FREE
NUT-FREE
ONE-POT
VEGETARIAN

PREP TIME:
15 minutes

COOK TIME:
30 minutes

SERVES 4

Greek-Inspired Veggie and Chickpea Sheet Pan Meal

There is nothing like a sheet pan to whip up an easy meal. You'll cook the potatoes and peppers in the oven first because their textures are firmer than the zucchini. Be sure to cut your zucchini into large 1-inch chunks so they don't get mushy. I recommend adding a dollop of garlic-yogurt sauce from the Roasted Eggplant recipe (page 94) on top. It's an amazingly flavorful combination!

1 pound red potatoes, cut into ½-inch pieces

1 large red bell pepper, stemmed, seeded, and cut into 1-inch pieces

2 tablespoons olive oil, divided

¼ teaspoon coarse kosher salt

1 (15-ounce) can low-sodium chickpeas, drained and rinsed

1 large zucchini, cut into 1-inch pieces

¼ cup chopped fresh dill

⅓ cup coarsely chopped pitted Kalamata olives

⅓ cup crumbled feta

2 teaspoons lemon juice

1. Preheat the oven to 425°F. Line a sheet pan with a silicone baking mat or parchment paper.

2. Place the potatoes on one half of the sheet pan and the peppers on the other. Drizzle 1 tablespoon of oil over the veggies and sprinkle with the salt. Toss to coat, but keep the potatoes and peppers separate. Spread the veggies out as much as possible.

3. Roast for 10 minutes. Add the chickpeas, zucchini, and the remaining 1 tablespoon of oil and carefully toss everything together. Spread the veggies out in an even layer and place back in the oven for 20 minutes, or until the zucchini is tender but not mushy.

4. Add the dill, olives, feta, and lemon juice and toss to combine. Taste, and add more lemon juice, if desired.

5. Serve warm.

VARIATION TIP: There are so many ways to change up the flavors of this dish. For example, you could add spices such as cumin or smoked paprika when you toss the veggies with oil. Or, you could add fresh elements after cooking, such as chopped avocado, walnuts, or pepitas.

PER SERVING: Calories: 303; Total fat: 15g; Saturated fat: 3g; Sodium: 404g; Total carbohydrates: 36g; Sugar: 5g; Fiber: 6g; Protein: 9g; Calcium: 94mg

PREP TIME:
10 minutes

COOK TIME:
20 minutes

SERVES 4

Whole-Grain Penne with Creamy Tofu "Ricotta" Tomato Sauce

Tofu is a versatile plant-based protein and the perfect ingredient to make a creamy vegan sauce for pasta. This tofu ricotta, adapted from my friend Chef Rachel Paghunasan, pairs well with the tangy tomato, pungent garlic, spicy red chili flakes, and aromatic basil. I prefer to use whole-wheat pasta because of its higher fiber content, but you can use any pasta that you have on hand. Feel free to add more chili flakes if you like extra heat.

8 ounces dried penne pasta
16 ounces firm tofu, drained
1 tablespoon lemon juice
1 tablespoon nutritional yeast
1 teaspoon onion powder
¾ teaspoon coarse kosher salt, divided

1 (14.5-ounce) can no-salt-added diced tomatoes
1 tablespoon olive oil
⅛ teaspoon red chili flakes
1 teaspoon chopped garlic
½ cup packed coarsely chopped fresh basil leaves

1. Bring a large pot of water to a boil over high heat. Add penne and cook until al dente, about 12 minutes.

2. While waiting for the water to boil, make the tofu ricotta by crumbling the tofu into a blender. Add the lemon juice, nutritional yeast, onion powder, and ½ teaspoon of salt, and blend until smooth, scraping down the sides with a spatula as needed, about 30 seconds.

3. In a saucepan, mix together the tomatoes, oil, chili flakes, garlic, and the remaining ¼ teaspoon of salt and bring to a simmer over medium-low heat.

4. Once the pasta is done cooking, drain, and transfer to a 12-inch skillet over medium heat. Add the tofu ricotta and stir until the pasta is evenly coated. Add the tomato sauce mixture and stir until combined.

5. Spoon the mixture into shallow bowls and garnish each portion with about ¼ cup of basil. Serve immediately.

COOKING TIP: To estimate how much pasta to cook, remember that 2 ounces of dried pasta equals about ⅔ cup of cooked penne, ½ cup of cooked rotini, ¾ cup of cooked rigatoni, and 1 cup of cooked spaghetti.

PER SERVING: Calories: 326; Total fat: 9g; Saturated fat: 2g; Sodium: 381g; Total carbohydrates: 44g; Sugar: 4g; Fiber: 4g; Protein: 18g; Calcium: 267mg

PREP TIME:
10 minutes

COOK TIME:
20 minutes

SERVES 4

Seared Polenta with Sautéed Kale, Ricotta, and Pine Nuts

This recipe makes great use of traditionally Italian ingredients. Firm polenta sold in a tube is a convenience ingredient that can save a lot of time, and I highly recommend it. When preparing the kale for this dish, there's no need to use a knife. Just rip the leaves off the stems and into pieces. I generally buy whole-milk ricotta instead of the skim milk version because the texture is smoother and creamier and worth the extra calories and fat.

4 teaspoons olive oil, divided
1 large bunch lacinato or curly kale, stems discarded and leaves torn into pieces
⅛ teaspoon coarse kosher salt
2 tablespoons pine nuts

1 teaspoon red wine vinegar
1 (18-ounce) tube polenta, cut into ½-inch slices
1 cup whole-milk ricotta cheese
Freshly ground black pepper

1. Heat 2 teaspoons of oil in a 12-inch nonstick skillet over medium-high heat, until the oil is shimmering. Add the kale and cook for 3 minutes. Add the salt and pine nuts and stir until combined.

2. Cover the pan, leaving the lid ajar, and continue cooking, stirring halfway, for another 4 minutes. If the pine nuts start burning, turn the heat down.

3. Turn the heat off, add the vinegar, and stir. Transfer the kale to a dish and keep warm.

4. Heat the remaining 2 teaspoons of oil in the same pan over medium-high heat until the oil is hot. Add the polenta rounds and sear until a golden crust has formed, about 5 minutes on each side.

5. Place ½ cup of kale and 2 polenta rounds on each of four plates. Add ¼ cup of ricotta and a sprinkling of pepper to each serving.

6. Serve warm or at room temperature.

VARIATION TIP: If you like your dish a bit more saucy, warm up some prepared marinara sauce and spoon it over each serving.

PER SERVING: Calories: 276; Total fat: 17g; Saturated fat: 7g; Sodium: 371g; Total carbohydrates: 21g; Sugar: 1g; Fiber: 2g; Protein: 10g; Calcium: 171mg

PREP TIME:
5 minutes

COOK TIME:
25 minutes

SERVES 4

Roasted Veggie Tacos with Romesco Sauce

Roasted veggies are delicious alone, but Spanish romesco sauce really makes them shine, while landing this recipe firmly along the Mediterranean! I simplified the sauce to make it quick and easy, so you'll want to make this again and again. When heating the tortillas, I prefer to soften and slightly char them directly on a gas stove. It really adds an extra dimension of flavor, but you can also warm the tortillas in the microwave if that works better for you.

1½ pounds cremini mushrooms, cut into ½-inch-thick slices
2 pounds cauliflower, cut into 1½-inch pieces
3 tablespoons olive oil, divided
1 teaspoon dried oregano
¾ teaspoon coarse kosher salt, divided

¼ cup unsalted raw almonds
2 garlic cloves
6 ounces jarred roasted red peppers
¼ cup canned fire-roasted tomatoes
½ teaspoon smoked paprika
1 teaspoon red wine vinegar
12 corn tortillas

1. Preheat the oven to 450°F. Line two sheet pans with a silicone baking mat or parchment paper.

2. Place the mushrooms on one pan and the cauliflower on the other. To each pan add 1 tablespoon of oil, ½ teaspoon of oregano, ¼ teaspoon of salt, and toss them until evenly coated. Spread out the veggies in one layer. Place the pan with the cauliflower on the bottom rack and the pan with the mushrooms on the upper rack and roast for 22 minutes, or until the veggies are tender.

3. While the veggies are roasting, combine the almonds and garlic in the bowl of a food processor and process until the mixture looks like coarse sand. Add the peppers, tomatoes, smoked paprika, the remaining ¼ teaspoon of salt, vinegar, and the remaining 1 tablespoon of oil and process until smooth.

4. To heat the tortillas on a gas stove, place 1 tortilla directly onto the burner of the stove, over a medium flame for 15 seconds. Flip the tortilla over and cook for another 15 seconds, or until you see small charred spots on the tortilla. Place the tortilla on plate and cover with a towel to keep warm. Repeat with the remaining tortillas.

5. Place 3 tortillas on each of four plates. Place ¼ cup of each veggie on top of each tortilla. Spoon 1 heaping tablespoon of romesco sauce over each veggie-topped tortilla. Serve immediately.

COOKING TIP: If you don't have a gas stove, you can also warm the tortillas in the microwave. Place a stack of 4 tortillas on a microwave-safe plate, cover with a damp paper towel, and microwave on high in 30-second intervals, until warmed. Repeat with the remaining tortillas.

PER SERVING: Calories: 374; Total fat: 18g; Saturated fat: 2g; Sodium: 567g; Total carbohydrates: 50g; Sugar: 9g; Fiber: 11g; Protein: 10g; Calcium: 115mg

PREP TIME:
10 minutes

COOK TIME:
20 minutes

SERVES 4

Roasted Eggplant with Za'atar Chickpeas and Garlic-Yogurt Sauce

In order to keep the total time for this recipe at 30 minutes, I used small, narrow eggplants that only need to be halved, so they will cook faster. Both Chinese and Japanese eggplants are purple, though the Japanese variety tend to be darker. Supermarkets usually have one or the other, so the eggplant shouldn't be difficult to find. I recommend serving a simple green salad on the side.

3 tablespoons olive oil, divided

1½ pounds Japanese or Chinese eggplant, stem removed and halved vertically

¾ teaspoon coarse kosher salt, divided

1 cup plain low-fat (2 percent) Greek yogurt

½ teaspoon garlic powder

1 tablespoon lemon juice

1 (15-ounce) can low-sodium chickpeas

2 teaspoons ground sumac

1 teaspoon dried thyme

2 teaspoons sesame seeds

1. Preheat the oven to 425°F. Line a sheet pan with a silicone baking mat or parchment paper.

2. Pour 1 tablespoon of oil on the sheet pan and roll the eggplant in the oil, using your hands to coat both sides. Sprinkle the cut side with ¼ teaspoon of salt and place the eggplant cut-side down on the sheet pan. Roast for 15 minutes, or until tender.

3. While the eggplant is cooking, in a medium bowl, mix together the yogurt, garlic powder, lemon juice, 1 tablespoon of oil, and ¼ teaspoon of salt. Set aside.

4. Heat the remaining 1 tablespoon of oil in a 10-inch nonstick skillet over medium-high heat until the oil is shimmering. Add the chickpeas, sumac, thyme, sesame seeds, and the remaining ¼ teaspoon of salt and stir until the chickpeas are coated. Cook without stirring for 2 minutes. Stir, then cook without stirring for another 2 minutes.

5. Place 2 eggplant halves on each of two plates, top with chickpeas and garlic-yogurt sauce, and serve.

6. Serve warm.

PER SERVING: Calories: 237; Total fat: 14g; Saturated fat: 2g; Sodium: 459g; Total carbohydrates: 22g; Sugar: 7g; Fiber: 6g; Protein: 10g; Calcium: 105mg

PREP TIME:
15 minutes

COOK TIME:
40 minutes

SERVES 6

Lebanese-Inspired Rice and Lentils with Caramelized Onions and Peppers

Did you know that you can freeze cooked legumes and grains? They hold up wonderfully when frozen and come in handy when you just don't feel like making a side dish from scratch. The inspiration for this dish is mujadara, a Lebanese lentil and rice dish with caramelized or crispy onions. I included red pepper to add more veggie variety.

2 tablespoons olive
  oil, divided
5 cups thinly sliced
  yellow onion
2 red bell peppers, stemmed,
  seeded, and thinly sliced
¾ cup long-grain brown rice
3 cups water

¾ teaspoon coarse kosher
  salt, divided
¾ cup brown lentils
⅔ cup chopped fresh parsley
½ teaspoon honey
½ teaspoon ground cumin
½ ground coriander
Small pinch ground cinnamon

1. Heat 1 tablespoon of oil in a 12-inch nonstick skillet over medium-high heat until the oil is shimmering. Add the onions and peppers and cook, stirring often, for 5 minutes. Cover the pan with a lid, leaving it slightly ajar, lower the heat to medium, and cook, stirring occasionally, about 30 minutes, or until the rice and lentils are also done cooking.

2. Place the rice, water, and ½ teaspoon of salt in a saucepan over high heat and bring to a boil. Cover, lower the heat to low, and simmer for 15 minutes.

3. Add the lentils to the rice, stir, cover, and cook until tender, about 15 minutes. If there is a little bit of water still in the pan after the rice and lentils are tender, remove the lid and cook until the liquid evaporates, 2 to 3 minutes. Stir in the parsley and the remaining 1 tablespoon of oil.

4. Add the remaining ¼ teaspoon of salt, honey, cumin, coriander, and cinnamon to the peppers and onions, stir until combined, and cook for an additional 5 minutes.

5. Divide the lentils and rice mixture among four bowls and top with the peppers and onions.

STORAGE TIP: After cooling, place any leftovers into an airtight container or zip-top plastic bag and freeze for up to 6 months.

PER SERVING: Calories: 271; Total fat: 6g; Saturated fat: 1g; Sodium: 255g; Total carbohydrates: 45g; Sugar: 7g; Fiber: 10g; Protein: 11g; Calcium: 56mg

DAIRY-FREE
5-INGREDIENT
30-MINUTE
VEGAN

PREP TIME:
15 minutes

COOK TIME:
10 minutes

SERVES 4

Gnocchi with Broccoli Rabe, Sun-Dried Tomatoes, and Pine Nuts

Who doesn't love a main course that requires only five ingredients? I love the texture of broccoli rabe, but feel free to use any of your favorite vegetables. This is a great clean-out-the-refrigerator kind of meal if you have a veggie that is almost past its prime. Feel free to use broccoli if your store doesn't carry broccoli rabe. If you aren't dairy-free or vegan, a sprinkling of Parmesan or Romano cheese is a great addition.

½ cup julienned sun-dried tomatoes in olive oil, with 2 teaspoons plus 2 tablespoons of the oil reserved

10 ounces broccoli rabe, cut into 1-inch pieces

2 large scallions, white and green parts, chopped

1 (17.6-ounce) package prepared gnocchi

¼ cup pine nuts

½ teaspoon coarse kosher salt

1. Bring a large saucepan of water to a boil over high heat.

2. While the water is coming to a boil, heat 2 teaspoons of oil in a 12-inch nonstick skillet over medium-high heat until the oil is shimmering. Add the broccoli rabe, scallions, and sun-dried tomatoes and cook, stirring often, until the broccoli rabe is tender but still has a little bite, 5 to 6 minutes.

3. Add the gnocchi to the boiling water and cook according to the package directions, usually about 3 minutes. Drain the gnocchi and add to the veggies in the skillet, along with the pine nuts.

4. Add the remaining 2 tablespoons of oil and the salt to the skillet and stir until combined. Cook until heated through, about 1 minute.

5. Serve warm.

VARIATION TIP: For added plant protein, add ¾ cup of cooked brown lentils with the veggies. If you don't want to cook the lentils, you can also soak ¼ cup of raw lentils overnight. Drain, then throw them in the skillet when you add the broccoli rabe. I don't recommend canned lentils for this dish because they tend to be very mushy.

PER SERVING: Calories: 407; Total fat: 17g; Saturated fat: 3g; Sodium: 305g; Total carbohydrates: 57g; Sugar: 1g; Fiber: 7g; Protein: 8g; Calcium: 62mg

PREP TIME:
15 minutes

COOK TIME:
45 minutes

SERVES 6

Veggie Paella with Edamame and Artichokes

Paella is one of the most well-known dishes found in Spain. Most often, it contains seafood, chicken, or chorizo, but I've made a vegan version here with a variety of Mediterranean vegetables. It's easy to make, and you don't need a special pan to create your own at home. The best rice for paella is Spanish bomba. If you can find it, great, but if it's not at your local supermarket, Italian Arborio, traditionally used for risotto, is a fine substitute.

**3 cups low-sodium
vegetable stock**
**½ teaspoon saffron threads
(optional)**
1 tablespoon olive oil
1 cup chopped onion
1 teaspoon chopped garlic
**1 red bell pepper, stemmed,
seeded, and thinly sliced**
**½ large fennel bulb,
thinly sliced**
1 large tomato, chopped

**1½ teaspoons
smoked paprika**
**¾ teaspoon coarse
kosher salt**
**1½ cups Spanish bomba or
Arborio rice**
**2 cups frozen shelled
edamame, thawed**
**1 (12-ounce) jar marinated
artichoke hearts, drained
and halved**
**Lemon wedges, for serving
(optional)**

1. Preheat the oven to 400°F.

2. In a saucepan over low heat, warm the broth and saffron (if using).

3. Heat the oil in a 12-inch oven-safe skillet over medium-high heat until the oil is shimmering. Add the onion, garlic, peppers, and fennel and cook, stirring occasionally, for 5 minutes. Add the tomato, smoked paprika, and salt and cook, stirring occasionally, for another 5 minutes.

4. Add the rice, stir until coated, and cook for 2 minutes.

5. Add the edamame and saffron broth, raise the heat to high, and bring to a boil. Cook until the mixture is no longer soupy, about 8 minutes. Do not stir during this time.

6. Place the pan in the oven and bake for 15 minutes. Remove the pan from oven, evenly distribute the artichoke hearts over the paella, cover, and let sit for 10 minutes.

7. Serve warm with lemon wedges (if using).

PER SERVING: Calories: 318; Total fat: 5g; Saturated fat: 1g; Sodium: 442g; Total carbohydrates: 58g; Sugar: 7g; Fiber: 6g; Protein: 12g; Calcium: 333mg

PREP TIME:
15 minutes,
plus
30 minutes
to marinate

COOK TIME:
40 minutes

SERVES 4

Roasted Tofu, Sweet Potato, and Broccoli Bowl with Tahini Sauce and Avocado

If you think you don't like tofu, I dare you to give it another chance and try this recipe. By marinating the tofu and baking it in the oven, it comes out browned, pleasantly chewy, and flavorful. There's a ton of plant nutrition packed into this bowl, including protein, healthy fats, fiber, beta-carotene, and magnesium.

1 (16-ounce) package extra-firm tofu, cut into ¾-inch cubes

2 tablespoons lemon juice

1 teaspoon olive oil, plus 1 tablespoon

1 teaspoon garlic powder, plus ¼ teaspoon

½ teaspoon plus ⅛ teaspoon coarse kosher salt, divided

1 pound sweet potatoes, peeled and cut into ¼-inch-thick slices

12 ounces broccoli, cut into 1½-inch pieces

2 tablespoons unsalted tahini

3 tablespoons water, plus more if needed

1 small avocado, diced

2 tablespoons plus 2 teaspoons green pumpkin seeds (also sold as pepitas)

1. In a large bowl, combine the tofu, lemon juice, 1 teaspoon of oil, 1 teaspoon of garlic powder, and ¼ teaspoon of salt and toss gently until combined. Marinate for 30 minutes.

2. Preheat the oven to 400°F. Line two sheet pans with silicone baking mats or parchment paper.

3. Transfer the tofu to one of the sheet pans, making sure to let any excess marinade drip back into the bowl. Place the sweet potato and broccoli on the second sheet pan and toss with the remaining 1 tablespoon of oil and ¼ teaspoon of salt. If the pan is too crowded, move some of the veggies to the pan with the tofu.

4. Bake for 20 minutes, or until the veggies are tender. Flip the tofu over and transfer the veggies to a large bowl. If the sweet potatoes aren't tender enough, leave those in for another 5 minutes. Continue baking the tofu for an additional 20 minutes, or until the tofu is browned around the edges.

5. In a small bowl, whisk together the tahini, remaining ¼ teaspoon of garlic powder, and remaining ⅛ teaspoon of salt. Whisk in 1 tablespoon of water at a time until all 3 tablespoons of water have been incorporated and a thin sauce has formed. Add more water if it seems too thick.

6. Divide the tofu, sweet potatoes, and broccoli among four bowls. Top with avocado, pepitas, and drizzle with the tahini sauce.

7. Serve warm or at room temperature.

INGREDIENT TIP: Be sure to purchase extra-firm tofu and not silken tofu, which is at the opposite end of the texture spectrum and used for recipes like smoothies and puddings. If you find super-firm tofu, you can use that as well.

PER SERVING: Calories: 354; Total fat: 22g; Saturated fat: 3g; Sodium: 355g; Total carbohydrates: 26g; Sugar: 5g; Fiber: 8g; Protein: 18g; Calcium: 149mg

PREP TIME:
45 minutes

COOK TIME:
35 minutes

SERVES 4

Stuffed Grape Leaves with Bulgur, Lentils, and Dill

There is definitely an art to stuffing grape leaves, but after the first few you'll get the hang of it. The taste of homemade stuffed grape leaves, sometimes called dolmas, is so much fresher than any canned version. The key is not to overfill the leaves with stuffing and to roll the leaves up tightly like mini burritos. Because the leaves are different sizes, you'll need to use your best judgment in deciding how much filling each leaf can handle. If you rip some of the leaves, don't worry because there are plenty of leaves in the jar. Better to have too many than not enough!

1 (1-pound) jar grape leaves in brine
¾ cup brown or green lentils
1 cup coarse bulgur
1 cup chopped fresh dill
¼ cup lemon juice, plus 2 tablespoons

3 tablespoons olive oil
½ teaspoon coarse kosher salt
Pinch freshly ground black pepper

1. Place the grape leaves in a colander, drain, and rinse. Leave to drain while preparing the filling.

2. Place 2 cups of water and the lentils in a saucepan over high heat and bring to a boil. Lower the heat to low, cover, and simmer for 3 minutes. Add the bulgur, stir, and cover the saucepan again. Let cook for 6 minutes. It's okay if the lentils aren't cooked all the way. They will continue cooking when the stuffed grape leaves are cooked.

3. Transfer the lentils and bulgur to a large bowl, add the dill, ¼ cup of lemon juice, oil, salt, and pepper and stir until combined. Taste, and add more salt and lemon juice, if desired.

4. Set up a rolling station with a platter and a clean cutting board next to the bowl of filling. Place 1 grape leaf, vein-side up with the stem end closest to you, at the bottom of the cutting board. Place about 2 tablespoons of filling (depending on how big the leaf is) in the center of the leaf, right above the stem end. Fold the sides over the filling and roll tightly toward the top of the cutting board, like you're rolling a burrito or spring roll. Keep tucking the sides in as you roll up. Place the stuffed grape leaf on the platter and repeat until you have rolled 24 leaves. Set aside any ripped leaves to use for covering the bottom of the pan.

5. Line the bottom of a 12-inch skillet or pot with grape leaves. Place as many of the stuffed grape leaves in the pan as possible in one layer, seam-side down. You may need to cook them in batches.

6. In a bowl, mix together 2 cups of water and the remaining 2 tablespoons of lemon juice and pour it over the stuffed leaves. Bring to a boil over high heat. Place a lid on the pan, lower the heat to low, and cook for 35 minutes, or until the liquid has been mostly absorbed.

7. Using tongs, carefully remove the stuffed leaves from the pan, taking care not to unwrap them. Serve hot or at room temperature.

INGREDIENT TIP: Don't skip rinsing and draining the grape leaves. Jarred grape leaves contain a high amount of sodium, and rinsing and draining will help remove some of it.

PER SERVING (6 STUFFED LEAVES): Calories: 212; Total fat: 7g; Saturated fat: 1g; Sodium: 526g; Total carbohydrates: 25g; Sugar: 1g; Fiber: 7g; Protein: 7g; Calcium: 20mg

PREP TIME:
10 minutes

COOK TIME:
20 minutes

SERVES 4

Quick Socca with Roasted Cherry Tomatoes and Cannellini Beans

Socca is a traditional savory chickpea pancake from Nice, in the South of France. In this gorgeous seaside city, you'll often see cooks at outdoor markets making socca in huge cast-iron pans. It's a must-try if you ever visit! Although we can't quite achieve the same texture of socca in our home kitchens, we can still use authentic ingredients to make an absolutely delicious dish. Serve it with a big green salad.

1 cup chickpea flour
½ teaspoon coarse kosher salt, divided
Pinch freshly ground black pepper
1 cup water
3 tablespoons olive oil, divided

1 pound cherry tomatoes, halved
1 (15-ounce) can low-sodium cannellini beans, drained and rinsed
1 teaspoon herbes de Provence
¼ cup chopped fresh chives

1. In a medium bowl, mix together the chickpea flour, ¼ teaspoon of salt, and the pepper. Pour in the water and 1 tablespoon of oil and whisk until the mixture is smooth. Set aside.

2. Preheat the oven to 450°F. Line a sheet pan with a silicone baking mat or parchment paper.

3. Place the tomatoes and beans on the prepared sheet pan. Add the herbes de Provence, 1 tablespoon of oil, and the remaining ¼ teaspoon of salt and toss until combined. Spread out the mixture on the pan and roast on the top rack of the oven for 20 minutes, shaking the pan halfway through.

4. As soon as you put the tomatoes in the oven, heat the remaining 1 tablespoon of oil in an ovenproof 12-inch skillet over high heat. Swirl the oil to coat the pan, add the socca batter and swirl to make sure the batter spreads out evenly. Place the skillet on the bottom rack in the oven and bake for 15 minutes, or until the edges are golden brown and crispy.

5. Remove the tomato mixture from the oven and toss with the chives directly on the pan. The tomatoes should look soft, but still have some shape.

6. Cut the socca into 4 pieces and place each one on a plate. Top each piece with the tomatoes and beans, and serve immediately.

COOKING TIP: If you have the time, let the batter rest for 30 minutes to 12 hours. You can also add chopped herbs and garlic to the batter, if you like, for some added flavor. If your pan is smaller than 12 inches, make the socca in two batches so the pancake isn't too thick.

PER SERVING: Calories: 244; Total fat: 12g; Saturated fat: 2g; Sodium: 284g; Total carbohydrates: 26g; Sugar: 6g; Fiber: 7g; Protein: 9g; Calcium: 285mg

Shrimp Scampi
Pasta, *page 126*

Fish and Shellfish

DAIRY-FREE
5-INGREDIENT
GLUTEN-FREE
NUT-FREE
30-MINUTE

PREP TIME:
10 minutes

COOK TIME:
20 minutes

SERVES 4

Broiled Catfish with Sautéed Red Onions, Spinach, and Grapes

If you've never sautéed or roasted grapes, you must try it. Roasted grapes sweetly complement to many protein and veggie dishes. Adding the vinegar at the end of cooking creates a sweet-and-sour flavor similar to an Italian condiment called *agrodolce*, which literally means "sour and sweet." The grape, onion, and spinach mixture would also pair well with pork or chicken.

1 tablespoon olive oil, divided
½ large red onion,
   thinly sliced
1½ cups red grapes
5 ounces baby
   spinach leaves
½ teaspoon coarse kosher
   salt, divided

2 pinches freshly ground
   pepper, divided
1½ teaspoons red
   wine vinegar
1¼ pounds catfish fillets

1. Preheat the oven to the high broiler setting. Line a broiler pan or sheet pan with aluminum foil.

2. Heat 2 teaspoons of oil in a 12-inch nonstick skillet over medium-high heat until the oil is shimmering. Add the onion and grapes and cook for 10 minutes. Add the spinach, ¼ teaspoon of salt, and a pinch of pepper, and cook until the spinach is wilted, about 2 minutes. Stir in the vinegar, taste, and add more, if desired.

3. Spread out the remaining 1 teaspoon of oil on the foil-lined pan. Pat the fish fillets dry, place them in the pan, and rub them in the oil on both sides, until coated. Sprinkle the fish with the remaining ¼ teaspoon of salt and a pinch of pepper. Broil for 6 to 8 minutes, or until fish is flaky and golden brown.

4. Divide the grape mixture among four plates and top with the fish, pouring any remaining juices from the grapes over the top.

5. Serve warm.

VARIATION TIP: Other types of fish that are well suited for the broiler are sole, tilapia, snapper, or trout.

PER SERVING: Calories: 239; Total fat: 12g; Saturated fat: 2g; Sodium: 364g; Total carbohydrates: 15g; Sugar: 11g; Fiber: 2g; Protein: 18g; Calcium: 54mg

PREP TIME:
10 minutes

COOK TIME:
25 minutes

SERVES 6

Salmon, Sweet Potato, and White Bean Cakes

These patties should really be called superfood cakes because they contain three of the healthiest foods on the planet: salmon, sweet potatoes, and white beans. Among these three ingredients, you have heart-healthy fats, fiber, and tons of vitamins and minerals. I recommend serving this dish with Smoked Paprika Aioli (page 168).

9 ounces red garnet sweet potato
1 (15-ounce) can low-sodium cannellini beans, drained and rinsed
2 (6-ounce) cans boneless, skinless salmon, drained
1½ teaspoons Dijon mustard
1 cup chopped scallions

⅓ cup chopped fresh dill
½ cup panko bread crumbs
½ teaspoon coarse kosher salt
Pinch freshly ground black pepper
1 egg
2 tablespoons olive oil, divided

1. Prick the sweet potato multiple times with a fork and microwave on high for 5 minutes. If not tender, continue to microwave in 1-minute increments. Cut a big slit through the skin and let cool.

2. In a large bowl, mash the beans with a potato masher or fork. Add the salmon, mustard, scallions, dill, panko, salt, pepper, and egg and mix until combined.

3. Peel the sweet potato. Place the flesh in a small bowl, mash with a fork, and transfer to the large bowl with the beans. Using your hands, mix together the ingredients until combined. Form the mixture into 12 equal-size cakes.

4. Heat 1 tablespoon of oil in a 12-inch nonstick skillet over medium-high heat until the oil is shimmering. Add enough cakes to fit in the pan comfortably, about 7, and cook for 4 minutes. Flip the cakes over and cook until browned, about 4 minutes. Transfer the cakes to a plate.

5. If cooking in batches, wipe out the skillet, add the remaining 1 tablespoon of oil, and cook until browned on both sides.

6. Serve warm.

STORAGE TIP: The uncooked cakes can be frozen. Line a sheet pan with parchment paper, place the cakes on the pan, and freeze. Once the cakes are frozen, transfer them to an airtight container or zip-top plastic bag and freeze for up to 6 months. To cook the cakes, bake in a 350°F oven for 30 minutes, flipping halfway. Alternatively, cook the cakes in an oiled skillet over medium heat for about 6 minutes per side.

PER SERVING: Calories: 211; Total fat: 9g; Saturated fat: 2g; Sodium: 327g; Total carbohydrates: 21g; Sugar: 4g; Fiber: 4g; Protein: 14g; Calcium: 289mg

PREP TIME:
15 minutes

COOK TIME:
10 minutes

SERVES 4

Pan-Seared Salmon with Chopped Salad

Don't you love a nice piece of restaurant-cooked salmon with that crispy golden-brown sear? You can actually make it at home, and it's easy! All you need is a hot pan, some oil, and 10 minutes. Serve the salmon and salad with a whole-grain side such as steamed brown rice, quinoa, or Farro Pilaf (page 60).

1½ pounds boneless salmon fillets, cut into 4 portions
½ teaspoon coarse kosher salt, divided
Pinch freshly ground black pepper
1 tablespoon olive oil, plus 2 teaspoons
4 ounces English or Persian cucumber, cut into ¼-inch pieces

6 ounces cherry tomatoes, quartered
4 large radishes, cut into ¼-inch pieces
1 tablespoon lemon juice
3 scallions, white and green parts, chopped
¼ cup chopped fresh mint leaves

1. Pat the salmon dry with paper towels and sprinkle ¼ teaspoon of salt and the pepper over the fish.

2. Heat 1 tablespoon of oil in a 12-inch nonstick skillet over medium-high heat until the oil is shimmering. Add the salmon fillets, skin-side down if the fillets have skin. Cook for 4 minutes. Flip the fish over with a spatula and cook until the fish flakes and is cooked through, another 3 to 4 minutes.

3. In a medium bowl, combine the remaining 2 teaspoons of oil, cucumber, tomatoes, radishes, lemon juice, onions, mint, and the remaining ¼ teaspoon of salt. Taste, and add more lemon juice, if desired.

4. Serve about ⅔ cup of the salad with each piece of salmon.

PER SERVING: Calories: 255; Total fat: 13g; Saturated fat: 2g; Sodium: 358g; Total carbohydrates: 4g; Sugar: 2g; Fiber: 1g; Protein: 33g; Calcium: 33mg

Baked Lemon-Garlic Salmon in Foil Packets

I hate spending money on salmon and then accidentally over-cooking it. Baking salmon in a foil pouch helps avoid that because the fish steams in the packet and will retain its moisture. This type of preparation also works well with any meaty white fish, such as halibut. Get a good whiff when you unwrap the pouches because the aroma of lemon and garlic is divine.

Zest and juice of 1 lemon
1 tablespoon minced garlic
1 tablespoon olive oil, plus
  1 teaspoon
1¼ pounds boneless salmon
  fillet, cut into 4 portions

¼ teaspoon coarse kosher salt
Pinch freshly ground
  black pepper
12 thin slices lemon

DAIRY-FREE
5-INGREDIENT
GLUTEN-FREE
NUT-FREE
ONE-POT
30-MINUTE

PREP TIME:
10 minutes

COOK TIME:
20 minutes

SERVES 4

1. Preheat the oven to 375°F. Cut 4 (12-by-12-inch) pieces of aluminum foil.

2. In a small bowl, mix together the lemon zest, lemon juice, garlic, and 1 tablespoon of oil.

3. Spread ¼ teaspoon of oil over each piece of foil and place a portion of salmon on top. Sprinkle the salt and pepper over the salmon, spoon 1 tablespoon of the lemon-garlic mixture on each portion, and place 3 lemon slices on top of each fillet.

4. Seal the foil packets by pulling the bottom and top edges together, folding them over, and pinching well to seal. Fold the sides inward. Place the packets on a sheet pan and bake for 12 minutes.

5. Let the packets sit for 6 minutes before unwrapping. The salmon will continue to cook as it sits. Be careful to avoid the hot steam when opening the packets.

6. Transfer each portion of salmon to a plate and pour any lemon-garlic sauce over the fish. Serve hot.

PER SERVING: Calories: 231; Total fat: 11g; Saturated fat: 2g; Sodium: 230g; Total carbohydrates: 1g; Sugar: 0g; Fiber: 0g; Protein: 32g; Calcium: 17mg

PREP TIME:
5 minutes

COOK TIME:
25 minutes

SERVES 4

Sardines with Cherry Tomato and Caper Sauce

If you've never had sardines before, this is a great introduction to them. Boneless, skinless, canned sardines are a rich source of omega-3 fatty acids and a very budget-friendly seafood option. And they are so good! If you have any fresh basil on hand, add a few tablespoons just before serving. I recommend serving pasta with this dish, as the sauce coats the noodles well.

1 tablespoon olive oil
1 cup chopped shallot
1½ pounds cherry tomatoes, about half of them cut in half
3 tablespoons capers, drained, rinsed, and coarsely chopped
½ cup dry white wine

¼ cup water
⅛ teaspoon coarse kosher salt
Pinch freshly ground black pepper
4 (3.75-ounce) cans boneless, skinless sardines in olive oil, drained

1. Heat the oil in a 12-inch nonstick skillet over medium-high heat until the oil is shimmering. Add the shallots, tomatoes, and capers, and cook, stirring occasionally, about 15 minutes.

2. Add the wine, water, salt, and pepper, raise the heat to medium, stir, and simmer for 3 minutes. Nestle the sardines in the sauce and continue cooking until just heated through, about 3 minutes.

3. Carefully transfer the sardines to four plates. Top with the sauce and serve warm.

INGREDIENT TIP: A popular national brand that sells boneless, skinless sardines packed in olive oil that I like a lot is Crown Prince.

PER SERVING: Calories: 315; Total fat: 17g; Saturated fat: 4g; Sodium: 418g; Total carbohydrates: 14g; Sugar: 8g; Fiber: 4g; Protein: 22g; Calcium: 90mg

Baked Rockfish with Feta-Thyme Bread Crumbs

5-INGREDIENT
NUT-FREE
ONE-POT
30-MINUTE

PREP TIME:
10 minutes

COOK TIME:
15 minutes

SERVES 4

You can use other kinds of white fish for this recipe, including tilapia, sole, snapper, or catfish. If you use a thicker white fish, such as cod or halibut, you'll need to leave it in the oven for a few extra minutes. Don't leave out the squeeze of lemon after cooking. It adds a zesty bright flavor that balances the salty feta.

⅓ cup panko bread crumbs
⅓ cup crumbled feta cheese
2 teaspoons fresh thyme
**1 tablespoon olive oil, plus
  1 teaspoon**

1¼ pounds rockfish fillets
¼ teaspoon coarse kosher salt
4 lemon wedges

1. Preheat the oven to 400°F. Line a sheet pan with a silicone baking mat or parchment paper.

2. In a small bowl, mix together the panko, feta, thyme, and 1 tablespoon of oil.

3. Spread the remaining 1 teaspoon of oil over the sheet pan. Place the fish fillets on the pan and sprinkle with the salt. Evenly distribute the panko mixture over the fish and pat down.

4. Bake for 12 to 15 minutes, or until the fish easily flakes and the topping is slightly browned.

5. Squeeze 1 lemon wedge over each fillet and serve immediately.

INGREDIENT TIP: If you use frozen fish, be sure to thaw it and always dry the fish well with paper towels right before cooking to remove any excess water. This will help crisp the outside of the fish. If you skip this step, you may end up fish that becomes watery as it bakes.

PER SERVING: Calories: 204; Total fat: 9g; Saturated fat: 3g; Sodium: 378g; Total carbohydrates: 7g; Sugar: 1g; Fiber: 1g; Protein: 23g; Calcium: 94mg

PREP TIME:
15 minutes

COOK TIME:
15 minutes

SERVES 4

Black Cod with Cilantro, Lime, and Ginger

Black cod, sometimes called sablefish or butterfish, is truly one of my favorite fishes to work with, and it's a perfect fish for folks who worry about it drying out. Black cod is an oily fish, which makes it harder to overcook. If you have some extra time, marinate the fish in the herb rub for 30 minutes before baking.

1 cup packed chopped cilantro
2 scallions, white and green parts, coarsely chopped
Zest and juice of 1 lime
1 (1½-inch) piece fresh ginger, peeled and coarsely chopped

2 garlic cloves, peeled
2 teaspoons olive oil
1 tablespoon honey
1½ pounds black cod fillets, cut into 4 portions
⅛ teaspoon coarse kosher salt

1. Preheat the oven to 400°F. Line a sheet pan with a silicone baking mat or parchment paper.

2. Combine the cilantro, scallions, lime zest, lime juice, ginger, garlic, oil, and honey in a food processor and puree into a paste.

3. Coat the fish on both sides with the herb paste and place the fish skin-side down on the sheet pan. If there is herb paste on the pan, scoop it up and pat it on top of the fish. Sprinkle the salt equally over the fish.

4. Bake for 12 minutes, or until the fish easily flakes.

5. Divide the fish among four plates and serve.

VARIATION TIP: If your fish market doesn't have black cod, Chilean sea bass is the next best substitute. This fish fillet may be slightly thicker than black cod and may need a few more minutes to cook. Fish is done when it reaches an internal temperature of 145°F.

PER SERVING: Calories: 340; Total fat: 26g; Saturated fat: 5g; Sodium: 150g; Total carbohydrates: 7g; Sugar: 5g; Fiber: 1g; Protein: 21g; Calcium: 67mg

Braised Cod with Fennel, Tomatoes, and Butter Beans

DAIRY-FREE
GLUTEN-FREE
NUT-FREE
ONE-POT

PREP TIME:
10 minutes

COOK TIME:
25 minutes

SERVES 4

This dish can't be beat when it's a weeknight and you want to get dinner on the table fast. When buying seafood, purchase the best you can afford. Fish should always be as fresh as possible. If you can get it from a fish market, that's even better. Frozen fish is also acceptable. Be sure to defrost it in the refrigerator and cook it within 24 hours of thawing for the best results.

1 tablespoon olive oil

2 cups thinly sliced fennel

2 cups thinly sliced onion

1 teaspoon chopped garlic

1 tablespoon chopped fresh thyme

½ cup dry white wine

1 (15.5-ounce) can butter beans, drained and rinsed

½ cup water

1 pound boneless cod fillet, cut into 4 portions

½ teaspoon coarse kosher salt

2 teaspoons lemon juice, plus more, if desired

1. Heat the oil in a 12-inch nonstick skillet over medium-high heat until the oil is shimmering. Add the fennel, onion, garlic, and thyme and cook, stirring occasionally, for 10 minutes.

2. Add the wine and continue cooking for 1 minute. Add the beans and water and stir until combined. Nestle the cod fillets in the pan and sprinkle the salt over everything.

3. Cover the pan, leaving the lid slightly ajar, and cook until the fish is flaky and cooked through, about 10 minutes. Pour the lemon juice over the fish, taste, and add more, if desired.

4. Place a portion of fish into each of four shallow bowls. Divide the veggie mixture among the bowls and pour the broth over the top. Serve warm.

INGREDIENT TIP: If you can, I highly recommend getting your seafood from a community-supported fishery (CSF).

PER SERVING: Calories: 209; Total fat: 4g; Saturated fat: 1g; Sodium: 440g; Total carbohydrates: 17g; Sugar: 5g; Fiber: 5g; Protein: 20g; Calcium: 73mg

PREP TIME:
10 minutes

COOK TIME:
30 minutes

SERVES 4

Braised Moroccan-Inspired Sea Bass with Ras el Hanout and Olives

Ras el hanout is a fragrant spice blend that contains cinnamon, cloves, cumin, and cardamom (and sometimes many more). I've had good luck finding the Spicely or McCormick brands at my local grocer, but if your supermarket doesn't sell ras el hanout, try another Moroccan spice blend such as McCormick's harissa spice blend and add a pinch of cinnamon. This dish would be lovely served with Steamed Couscous with Golden Raisins and Pistachios (page 61).

2 tablespoons olive oil

½ large yellow onion, thinly sliced

1 medium red bell pepper, stemmed, seeded, and thinly sliced

1 teaspoon ras el hanout or other Moroccan spice blend

1 teaspoon paprika

2 tablespoons tomato paste

1 (14.5-ounce) can no-salt-added diced tomatoes

½ cup water

1 large zucchini, halved lengthwise, and cut into ¼-inch half-moons

1 cup chopped fresh cilantro

1 pound boneless, skinless sea bass, cut into 4 portions

½ teaspoon coarse kosher salt

⅓ cup pitted green olives, coarsely chopped

1. Heat the oil in a 12-inch nonstick skillet over medium-high heat until the oil is shimmering. Add the onions and peppers and cook, stirring occasionally, for 8 minutes.

2. Add the ras el hanout, paprika, and tomato paste and cook, stirring occasionally, for 2 minutes. Add the tomatoes and water, lower the heat to medium-low, and simmer for 5 minutes.

3. Add the zucchini and cilantro, stir until combined, and nestle the fish in the pan. Sprinkle the salt over the top, and cover, leaving the lid slightly ajar. Simmer for 15 minutes, using a spatula to flip the fish over halfway through.

4. Sprinkle the olives over the fish and serve warm.

COOKING TIP: If you're not sure when the oil in a pan is hot enough, wet your hand and flick a few drops of water into the pan. If the oil sizzles, you know it's hot enough.

PER SERVING: Calories: 291; Total fat: 11g; Saturated fat: 2g; Sodium: 339g; Total carbohydrates: 24g; Sugar: 14g; Fiber: 5g; Protein: 29g; Calcium: 102mg

**DAIRY-FREE
15-MINUTE
GLUTEN-FREE
NUT-FREE**

PREP TIME:
10 minutes

COOK TIME:
5 minutes

SERVES 4

Spice-Crusted Ahi with Mango-Cilantro Salsa

Ahi is a popular fish used in its raw form for poke and sushi, but it's also delicious when coated in spices and quickly seared on the outside just until a crust is formed, leaving the inside still raw. When serving raw fish, be sure to purchase from a reputable seafood purveyor. Tuna steaks are usually served rare because they often end up very dry when cooked all the way through.

2 teaspoons ground
  coriander
1 teaspoon caraway seeds
2 teaspoons garlic powder
1 teaspoon ground cumin
2 tablespoons sesame seeds
⅛ teaspoon freshly ground
  black pepper
1 pound ahi steaks, cut into
  4 portions

½ teaspoon coarse kosher
  salt, plus ⅛ teaspoon
2 tablespoons olive
  oil, divided
1 mango, peeled, pitted, and
  cut into ¼-inch pieces
⅓ cup chopped fresh cilantro
2 tablespoons lime juice

1. In a small bowl, mix together the coriander, caraway, garlic powder, cumin, sesame seeds, and pepper. Spread out the spice mixture on a dinner plate.

2. Pat the ahi dry with paper towels and sprinkle with ½ teaspoon of salt. Dip both sides of the fish into the spice mixture, thoroughly coating both sides.

3. Heat 1 tablespoon of oil in a 12-inch nonstick skillet over medium-high heat until the oil is shimmering. Place the fish in the hot oil and cook for 1½ minutes. Using a spatula, flip the fish over and continue to cook for another 1½ minutes. The outside should be seared, but the inside will be rare. Transfer to a plate and let the fish rest while you make the salsa.

4. In a medium bowl, mix together the mango, cilantro, lime juice, the remaining 1 tablespoon of oil, and the remaining ⅛ teaspoon of salt.

5. Cut the ahi into slices and divide them among four plates. Spoon the mango salsa over the fish and serve.

VARIATION TIP: Instead of serving with typical side dishes, the spice-crusted ahi and mango salsa would be delicious served over greens as a main course salad. The salsa has enough juice to act as a dressing, but you could add more lime and olive oil, if desired.

PER SERVING: Calories: 249; Total fat: 10g; Saturated fat: 2g; Sodium: 355g; Total carbohydrates: 10g; Sugar: 7g; Fiber: 2g; Protein: 30g; Calcium: 69mg

PREP TIME:
10 minutes

COOK TIME:
10 minutes

SERVES 4

Pan-Seared Halibut with Olive Tapenade

Popular in the South of France, tapenades are a dream condiment for olive lovers. I've simplified the number of ingredients in my version, but you can also add anchovies, capers, and lemon zest. A mix of green and black olives can be nice, too, but please don't use canned black olives because the flavor won't be right. If you're not an olive lover, you can also top this seared fish with Smoked Paprika Aioli (page 168) or Salsa Verde (page 167).

¾ cup pitted Kalamata olives
2 cups coarsely chopped
　　fresh parsley
2 garlic cloves, peeled
　　and halved
1 tablespoon lemon juice
1 tablespoon olive oil, divided

1¼ pounds halibut, cut into
　　4 portions
¼ teaspoon coarse
　　kosher salt
Pinch freshly ground
　　black pepper

1. Combine the olives, parsley, garlic, lemon juice, and 1 teaspoon of oil to a food processor and pulse about 5 times, or until it is chopped well and no large pieces remain.

2. Pat the fish dry with paper towels and season both sides with the salt and pepper.

3. Heat the remaining 2 teaspoons of oil in a 12-inch nonstick skillet over medium-high heat until the oil is shimmering. Add the fish fillets and cook for 4 minutes. Using a spatula, flip the fish over and continue cooking until the fish is flaky and cooked all the way through, 3 to 4 minutes.

4. Transfer the fish to four plates and spoon the tapenade on top. Serve warm.

COOKING TIP: If you don't want to break out the food processor, you can also make the tapenade by chopping the olive, garlic, and parsley.

PER SERVING: Calories: 254; Total fat: 14g; Saturated fat: 2g; Sodium: 431g; Total carbohydrates: 5g; Sugar: 0g; Fiber: 1g; Protein: 28g; Calcium: 55mg

Tuna-Stuffed Avocados

DAIRY-FREE
15-MINUTE
5-INGREDIENT
GLUTEN-FREE
NO-COOK
NUT-FREE

PREP TIME:
15 minutes

SERVES 4

When I'm in the mood for a light meal, tuna-stuffed avocados are my go-to. If I weren't sticking to just five ingredients in this dish, I might top the tuna with some thinly sliced pickled red onion. You could also add chopped celery, shallot, capers, olives, or pumpkin seeds for some crunch. I recommend serving with a side of whole-grain crackers to scoop up the avocado after you've eaten the tuna salad.

2 small ripe avocados, pitted and halved

3 (2.6-ounce) pouches water-packed reduced-sodium light tuna, drained

½ medium red bell pepper, stemmed, seeded, and cut into ¼-inch pieces

3 tablespoons chopped fresh basil

1 tablespoon lemon juice

¼ teaspoon coarse kosher salt

Pinch freshly ground black pepper

1. Scoop about 2 tablespoons of pulp out of each avocado half and transfer it to a medium bowl. This will create a deeper well for the tuna.

2. Add the tuna to the avocado pulp in the bowl and mash with a fork. Add the peppers, basil, lemon juice, salt, and pepper and stir until combined.

3. Fill each avocado cavity with ½ cup of the tuna salad and serve at room temperature.

COOKING TIP: This dish is extra tasty if you grill the avocados first. Preheat a charcoal or gas grill. Brush the cut side of an avocado with a small amount of olive oil and cook until you see grill marks, 2 to 3 minutes.

PER SERVING: Calories: 173; Total fat: 11g; Saturated fat: 2g; Sodium: 251g; Total carbohydrates: 7g; Sugar: 1g; Fiber: 5g; Protein: 14g; Calcium: 14mg

PREP TIME:
10 minutes

COOK TIME:
15 minutes

SERVES 4

Shrimp Scampi Pasta

You can't have shrimp scampi without lots and lots of garlic and lemon, which I have included in my recipe, too. After the pasta is done cooking, this dish comes together very quickly, so keep your prepped ingredients close by. If you want to cut down on sodium, find fresh shrimp that has not been previously frozen, as manufacturers soak shrimp in a salt solution during the freezing process.

8 ounces dried spaghetti
**2 tablespoons olive
  oil, divided**
**1 pound large shrimp, peeled
  and deveined**
2 tablespoons chopped garlic
½ cup chopped shallot
¼ teaspoon red chili flakes

½ cup white wine
Zest and juice of 2 lemons
**2 tablespoons
  unsalted butter**
**½ teaspoon coarse
  kosher salt**
½ cup chopped fresh parsley

1. Bring a large pot of water to a boil over high heat. Add the pasta and cook, stirring often, until al dente, about 8 minutes. Scoop out ¼ cup of the pasta water and set aside. Drain the pasta and set aside.

2. Heat 1 tablespoon of oil in a 12-inch skillet over medium-high heat until the oil is shimmering. Add the shrimp, garlic, shallot, and chili flakes and cook for 2 minutes. Using tongs, flip the shrimp, add the wine, lemon zest, and lemon juice and continue cooking for an another 4 minutes.

3. Add the butter, salt, parsley, pasta, and the remaining 1 tablespoon of oil and toss until evenly coated.

4. Serve warm.

INGREDIENT TIP: Parsley adds a grassy brightness to the pasta, but if you want even more herbal notes, try adding a couple of teaspoons of chopped fresh thyme leaves.

PER SERVING: Calories: 488; Total fat: 16g; Saturated fat: 5g; Sodium: 899g; Total carbohydrates: 54g; Sugar: 3g; Fiber: 4g; Protein: 28g; Calcium: 109mg

Shrimp Pita Pizza

If you crave pizza, using whole-grain pita bread is a good way to make a personal pizza that's much healthier than the pie found at your local pizza shop. To maximize flavor and time, marinate the shrimp before prepping the other ingredients. Balsamic glaze is easy to find at the supermarket, but if you want to make your own, follow the Variation Tip for the Caprese Salad with Balsamic Glaze (page 53). It adds a beautiful richness to your pizza.

PREP TIME:
15 minutes

COOK TIME:
15 minutes

SERVES 4

2 tablespoons olive oil, divided
2 tablespoons lemon juice
1 teaspoon garlic powder
¼ teaspoon red chili flakes
12 ounces large shrimp, peeled and deveined
4 whole-grain pita rounds

2 cups baby spinach
1 cup shredded mozzarella cheese
2 tablespoons grated Parmesan cheese
1 cup thinly sliced zucchini rounds
2 tablespoons balsamic glaze

1. Preheat the oven to 400°F.

2. In a medium bowl, mix together 2 teaspoons of oil, lemon juice, garlic powder, and chili flakes. Add the shrimp, toss to coat, and marinate for 10 minutes.

3. While the shrimp is marinating, place the pitas on a sheet pan. Spread 1 teaspoon of oil over each pita.

4. Divide the spinach equally among the pitas. Top with the mozzarella, Parmesan, and zucchini.

5. Divide the shrimp among the pitas and drizzle the marinade over the top.

6. Bake for 12 to 15 minutes, or until the cheese is melted and the shrimp is pink.

7. Drizzle the balsamic glaze over each pita. Cut each pizza into 4 pieces and serve immediately.

PER SERVING: Calories: 392; Total fat: 13g; Saturated fat: 4g; Sodium: 601g; Total carbohydrates: 45g; Sugar: 6g; Fiber: 5g; Protein: 27g; Calcium: 253mg

PREP TIME:
10 minutes

COOK TIME:
10 minutes

SERVES 4

White Wine–Steamed Mussels with Garlic, Lemon, and Parsley

When purchasing mussels for an entrée, a good rule of thumb is about 1 pound per person. This may seem like a lot, but each pound of mussels will yield about 4 ounces of meat, and you'll need to allow for discarding the mussels that are already open when you wash them. Serve with crusty French bread to sop up the garlicky juices.

4 pounds mussels
1 tablespoon olive oil
½ cup chopped shallot
4 teaspoons chopped garlic, divided
1 cup dry white wine

2 tablespoons unsalted butter
Zest and juice of 2 lemons
⅓ cup chopped fresh parsley
¼ teaspoon salt

1. Wash the mussels and remove any dirt. If there are any fibrous beards on the shell, pull them out, pulling toward the hinge on the shell. Discard any mussels that are open.

2. Heat the oil in a large wide-bottomed pot over medium heat until the oil is shimmering. Add the shallots and 2 teaspoons of garlic and cook for 2 minutes.

3. Add the mussels to the pot, stir, and add the wine. Cover and steam the mussels until they open, 4 to 5 minutes.

4. When all the mussels are open, using a slotted spoon, transfer the mussels to four serving bowls. Throw away any mussels that do not open.

5. Add the butter, lemon zest, lemon juice, parsley, salt, and the remaining 2 teaspoons of garlic to the pot and cook, stirring, until the butter melts, about 1 minute. Divide the broth among the four bowls.

6. Serve immediately along with a bowl for the empty shells.

INGREDIENT TIP: The majority of mussels are farm-raised, which is a good thing for the environment. They are stored in tanks before being shipped off to your local fish market and expel sand and grit when stored in those tanks, making it unnecessary for the consumer to soak the mussels at home. If you're unsure of the source of your mussels, ask your fishmonger.

PER SERVING: Calories: 364; Total fat: 15g; Saturated fat: 5g; Sodium: 588g; Total carbohydrates: 15g; Sugar: 2g; Fiber: 1g; Protein: 31g; Calcium: 62mg

Roasted Chicken
with Lemon and Garlic,
page 136

Chapter Eight

Poultry and Meat

Chicken Sausage, Kale, and Brown Rice Bowl with Tomato Broth

This homey and richly flavored soup with Mediterranean staples garlic, onion, olive oil, and tomato is especially satisfying during the colder months of the year. Pork sausage is popular in countries such as Italy, France, and Spain, but I used chicken sausage to make this dish a bit healthier. To save time in the kitchen, I call for instant brown rice in this recipe, and I cook it in the same pan as the rest of the dish, making this dish both a complete meal and a one-pan wonder. No need to wash extra bowls and pans.

2 teaspoons olive oil
4 fully cooked chicken sausage links, each cut into 6 diagonal slices
1½ cups chopped onion
2 teaspoons chopped garlic
1 large bunch lacinato or curly kale, stems removed and leaves torn into bite-size pieces

1 cup instant brown rice
3 cups low-sodium chicken broth
1 (15-ounce) can no-salt-added diced tomatoes
¼ teaspoon coarse kosher salt
Pinch freshly ground black pepper

1. Heat the oil in a 12-inch skillet over medium-high heat until the oil is shimmering. Add the sausage and cook until browned, about 3 minutes. Transfer the sausage to a plate.

2. Add the onion and garlic to the pan and cook for 2 minutes. Add the kale and cook, stirring often, until the kale is just tender, about 3 minutes.

3. Return the sausage to the pan, along with any juices that have collected on the plate. Add the rice, broth, tomatoes, salt, and pepper and stir until the rice is evenly distributed.

4. Increase the heat to high and bring to a boil. Cover, lower the heat to medium-low, and simmer until the rice is tender, about 10 minutes.

5. Divide the sausage and veggies among four bowls and the pour broth over the top. Serve warm.

INGREDIENT TIP: Be sure to check the ingredient list on the chicken sausage package if you need to avoid gluten or dairy because some sausages may contain those allergens. Also, if you need to watch your salt intake, compare different brands of sausages for their sodium content because the amounts can vary greatly.

PER SERVING: Calories: 343; Total fat: 11g; Saturated fat: 3g; Sodium: 600g; Total carbohydrates: 46g; Sugar: 11g; Fiber: 5g; Protein: 20g; Calcium: 110mg

PREP TIME:
10 minutes

COOK TIME:
10 minutes

SERVES 4

Pan-Seared Chicken with Shallot Yogurt

When I make shallot yogurt, my husband eats it straight out of the bowl! As it sits, even for just 5 minutes, the flavors of the shallot will mellow and create a delicious topping for your chicken. You can also use the yogurt as a topping for fish or a veggie and grain bowl or as the base for a savory yogurt parfait. When cooking boneless, skinless chicken breasts, I have found that covering the pan with a lid during the second half of cooking helps it retain its juices and stay moist.

1 cup low-fat (2 percent) plain Greek yogurt

⅓ cup minced shallot

2 tablespoons olive oil, divided

1 tablespoon lemon juice

¾ teaspoon coarse kosher salt, divided

2 pinches freshly ground black pepper, divided

1¼ pounds boneless, skinless chicken breast fillets or chicken breasts pounded to ¾ inch thick

1½ teaspoons ground coriander

1. In a medium bowl, mix together the yogurt, shallot, 1 tablespoon of oil, lemon juice, ¼ teaspoon of salt, and a pinch of pepper. Set aside.

2. Pat the chicken dry with paper towels and rub with the coriander, the remaining ½ teaspoon of salt, and pinch of pepper.

3. Heat the remaining 1 tablespoon of oil in a 12-inch nonstick skillet over medium-high heat until the oil is shimmering. Add the chicken and cook until golden, about 4 minutes. Flip over the chicken, lower the heat to medium-low, cover the pan, and cook until the chicken is golden and reaches an internal temperature of 165°F when probed with an instant-read thermometer, another 5 to 6 minutes. Let the chicken rest for 5 minutes.

4. Cut the chicken across the grain into slices and place on a platter. Top with the shallot-yogurt sauce and serve immediately.

VARIATION TIP: If you enjoy dark meat more than white meat, feel free to make this dish using chicken thighs. Whichever type of meat you like best, the healthiest option is to remove the skin before eating.

PER SERVING: Calories: 246; Total fat: 11g; Saturated fat: 2g; Sodium: 439g; Total carbohydrates: 6g; Sugar: 4g; Fiber: 1g; Protein: 30g; Calcium: 87mg

DAIRY-FREE
5-INGREDIENT
GLUTEN-FREE
NUT-FREE

PREP TIME:
10 minutes

**COOK
TIME:** 1 hour
10 minutes

SERVES 6

Roasted Chicken with Lemon and Garlic

I don't know what's more comforting than a simple roasted chicken. It's definitely a recipe everyone should have in their repertoire. The simple flavors of garlic, lemon, and olive oil bring to mind the flavors of Provence. Within the first 10 minutes of roasting, your home will have the delicious aroma of garlic wafting through the air. If your family doesn't eat all the chicken in one sitting, save any leftovers to add to a big salad the next day.

2 tablespoons olive oil
**10 garlic cloves, 3 peeled
    and minced, 7 skins on and
    smashed with a knife**
**1 teaspoon dried Italian herb
    seasoning**
**Zest and juice of 1 lemon,
    peels reserved**

**½ teaspoon coarse
    kosher salt**
**Pinch freshly ground
    black pepper**
**1 (5-pound) whole chicken,
    neck and giblets removed**

1. Preheat the oven to 450°F.

2. In a small bowl, combine the oil, the minced garlic, Italian seasoning, lemon zest, 2 tablespoons of lemon juice, salt, and pepper.

3. Place the chicken, breast-side up, in a roasting pan and pat dry with paper towels. Loosen the skin where the breast meat is. Rub the lemon mixture under the skin and all over the rest of the chicken.

4. Place the smashed garlic cloves and lemon peels inside of the chicken cavity.

5. Roast for 20 minutes. Lower the oven temperature to 375°F and continue roasting for 40 to 50 minutes, or until the juices run clear, the thigh meat is no longer pink, and the internal

temperature reads 165°F when probed near the inner thigh (not touching the bone) with an instant-read thermometer.

6. Pour the remaining 1 tablespoon of lemon juice over the chicken and let it rest for 10 to 15 minutes before carving into slices. Serve immediately.

COOKING TIP: You can use anything that resembles a roasting pan, including a Pyrex pan, ovenproof skillet, cast-iron skillet, or even a sheet pan (just be sure it has sides to hold in the juices).

PER SERVING: Calories: 281; Total fat: 14g; Saturated fat: 3g; Sodium: 266g; Total carbohydrates: 2g; Sugar: 0g; Fiber: 0g; Protein: 36g; Calcium: 31mg

PREP TIME:
10 minutes

COOK TIME:
25 minutes

SERVES 8

Turkey, Mushroom, Arugula, and Feta Orzo Skillet

Did you know that orzo is a type of pasta? It kind of looks like very large, flat grains of rice. This one-pot dish almost reminds me of risotto, and it's full of mushrooms, greens, and lean ground turkey. Orzo sizes can vary among brands; I use Barilla, which is on the smaller side. If you use a larger orzo, such as the one from Trader Joe's, you may need to cook it for an extra minute. If you don't have arugula, you can also use baby spinach.

1 tablespoon olive oil
2 cups chopped onion
2 teaspoons chopped garlic
1 pound sliced mushrooms
**1 pound 93-percent lean
 ground turkey**
⅓ cup tomato paste
1½ teaspoons ground cumin
**1½ teaspoons ground
 coriander**

**¾ teaspoon coarse
 kosher salt**
**1 (5-ounce) container
 baby arugula**
12 ounces dried orzo
4 cups water
**6 ounces crumbled
 feta cheese**

1. Heat the oil in a 3½-quart Dutch oven or straight-sided skillet over medium-high heat until the oil is shimmering. Add the onions, garlic, and mushrooms and cook, stirring occasionally, until the mushrooms are tender, about 10 minutes.

2. Add the ground turkey and cook, using a spatula to break up the meat until the turkey is almost cooked through and very little pink remains, 4 to 5 minutes.

3. Add the tomato paste, cumin, coriander, and salt, stir until combined, and cook for another 2 minutes. Add the arugula, stir, and cook until just wilted, about 1 minute.

4. Add the orzo and the water, stir until combined, increase the heat to high, and bring to a boil. Stir frequently to prevent the orzo from sticking to the bottom of the pan. Lower the heat to medium-low and simmer, stirring often, until most of the liquid is absorbed but it's still a little soupy looking and the orzo is al dente, 6 to 7 minutes. Don't worry if the orzo seems a little underdone as it will continue cook.

5. Stir in the feta and serve warm.

STORAGE TIP: To freeze, place the cooled food in an airtight container and freeze for up to 3 months.

PER SERVING: Calories: 272; Total fat: 12g; Saturated fat: 5g; Sodium: 430g; Total carbohydrates: 23g; Sugar: 4g; Fiber: 3g; Protein: 19g; Calcium: 147mg

PREP TIME:
10 minutes

COOK TIME:
30 minutes

SERVES 6

Turkey Bolognese

I can think of few sauces as satisfying as a hearty Bolognese pasta sauce. It's traditionally made with beef in Italy (and originates from the city of Bologna), though here I used lean ground turkey to reduce the amount of saturated fat. I do not recommend using extra-lean turkey because the cooked meat tends to dry out. I added lots of veggies, not only for taste and extra nutrients but also to stretch out the amount of meat, giving you more sauce for your money. Serve with cooked whole-grain pasta.

1 tablespoon olive oil
1 cup chopped onion
1 tablespoon chopped garlic
½ cup finely chopped celery
½ cup shredded carrots
8 ounces baby bella mushrooms, finely chopped
1 pound 93-percent lean ground turkey

1 tablespoon dried Italian herb seasoning
⅓ cup dry white wine
1 (28-ounce) can no-salt-added crushed tomatoes
¾ teaspoon coarse kosher salt

1. Heat the oil in a 12-inch skillet or Dutch oven over medium-high heat until the oil is shimmering. Add the onion, garlic, celery, carrots, and mushrooms and cook, stirring occasionally, until the mushrooms are tender, about 8 minutes.

2. Add the turkey and Italian seasoning, and cook, using a spatula to break up the meat, until the turkey is cooked through, 6 to 8 minutes.

3. Add the wine, tomatoes, and salt, lower the heat to medium, and simmer, stirring often, until the sauce has thickened slightly and is hot, about 10 minutes.

4. Serve hot over pasta.

STORAGE TIP: Once cooled, the turkey Bolognese sauce can be frozen in an airtight container for up to 6 months.

PER SERVING: Calories: 213; Total fat: 9g; Saturated fat: 2g; Sodium: 333g; Total carbohydrates: 6g; Sugar: 7g; Fiber: 4g; Protein: 19g; Calcium: 44mg

Chili-Rubbed Pork Tenderloin with Kiwi-Pomegranate Salsa

DAIRY-FREE
GLUTEN-FREE
NUT-FREE
30-MINUTE

PREP TIME:
10 minutes

COOK TIME:
20 minutes

SERVES 4

Fruit salsa is a terrific pairing with roasted meats. No need to make a mess seeding a whole pomegranate because the seeds, also known as arils, are sold year-round in the produce section at the supermarket where precut fruit is usually kept. If peaches are in season, they would make a delicious addition, as well.

½ teaspoon coarse kosher salt, divided
2 teaspoons chili powder
1 teaspoon garlic powder
1 tablespoon olive oil, divided
1 pound pork tenderloin, tough silver skin removed with a sharp knife

½ cup pomegranate seeds
2 kiwifruits, peeled and chopped
1 scallion, white and green parts, chopped
2 teaspoons lime juice

1. Preheat the oven to 500°F. Line a sheet pan with aluminum foil.

2. In a small bowl, mix together ¼ teaspoon of salt, chili powder, garlic powder, and 2 teaspoons of oil until it forms a paste. Rub the paste all over the pork.

3. Place the pork on the prepared sheet pan and roast for 10 minutes. Turn the tenderloin over and roast for another 8 minutes, or until the spices on the outside have darkened but not burned. It's fine if there are some charred-looking spots. Let the pork rest for at least 5 minutes.

4. While the pork is roasting, in a medium bowl, mix together the pomegranate seeds, kiwifruits, scallion, lime juice, remaining 1 teaspoon of oil, and remaining ¼ teaspoon of salt.

5. Cut the pork into slices and arrange on a platter. Top with the salsa and its juices.

6. Serve while the pork is still warm.

PER SERVING: Calories: 201; Total fat: 7g; Saturated fat: 2g; Sodium: 292g; Total carbohydrates: 12g; Sugar: 7g; Fiber: 2g; Protein: 23g; Calcium: 22mg

Spanish-Inspired Ground Pork and Greens Skillet

I really enjoy the Spanish preparation of sautéed greens with golden raisins, pine nuts, and vinegar, and adding some ground pork seemed like a good idea to turn it into an easy entrée. The raisins add a tasty pop of sweetness that pairs well with the smoked paprika. I recommend using lean ground pork instead of extra lean because pork can become really dry when cooked without a decent amount of fat. Serve over steamed quinoa or brown rice.

2 teaspoons olive oil
1 pound lean ground pork
1 cup chopped onion
2 teaspoons chopped garlic
1 bunch chard, stems cut into slices and leaves coarsely chopped (keep stems and leaves separate)
¼ cup pine nuts

¼ cup golden raisins
1 teaspoon smoked paprika
½ teaspoon dried thyme
¼ teaspoon coarse kosher salt
⅓ cup low-sodium chicken broth
1 tablespoon red wine vinegar

1. Heat the oil in a 12-inch nonstick skillet over medium-high heat until the oil is shimmering. Add the ground pork and cook, using a spatula to break up the meat, until it is no longer pink, 5 to 6 minutes.

2. Carefully drain most of the fat from the pan and transfer the cooked pork to a plate and set aside.

3. Add the onions, garlic, and chard stems to the pan and cook until the onions start to soften, about 3 minutes. Add the chard leaves, pine nuts, and raisins and cook until chard is wilted, 4 to 5 minutes.

4. Add the smoked paprika, thyme, salt, chicken broth, and cooked pork along with its juices to the pan and stir until combined. Cook until the pork is warmed through, about 2 minutes.

5. Add the vinegar and stir until combined.

6. Spoon the mixture onto plates and serve warm with your desired cooked grain.

PER SERVING: Calories: 316; Total fat: 20g; Saturated fat: 6g; Sodium: 277g; Total carbohydrates: 16g; Sugar: 8g; Fiber: 3g; Protein: 21g; Calcium: 65mg

PREP TIME:
10 minutes

COOK TIME:
15 minutes

SERVES 4

Seared Pork Chops with Mustard-Oregano Pan Sauce

Pork chops are a great time-saving protein because they cook so quickly. The best way to tell whether meat is cooked through is with an instant-read thermometer. If you don't have a thermometer and you're not sure if the pork is done, cut into it. If the juices run clear, the pork is cooked.

4 (4-ounce) boneless pork chops, about 1 inch thick
½ teaspoon coarse kosher salt, plus a pinch
Pinch freshly ground black pepper
1 tablespoon olive oil
2 teaspoons chopped garlic

⅓ cup chopped shallot
⅔ cup low-sodium chicken broth
1 tablespoon lemon juice
1 tablespoon Dijon mustard
1 teaspoon honey
1 teaspoon chopped fresh oregano

1. Pat the pork chops dry with a paper towel and rub both sides with ½ teaspoon of salt and a pinch of pepper.

2. Heat the oil in a 12-inch skillet over medium-high heat until the oil is shimmering. Add the pork chops and sear until browned, about 4 minutes. Flip the pork chops over and cook until browned, the meat gives a little when you press on it, or until the internal temperature reads 145°F, 3 to 5 minutes. Transfer the pork to a plate and let rest.

3. Lower the heat to medium and in the same pan, cook the garlic and shallot, stirring frequently, until browned and softened, about 2 minutes. Add the broth, lemon juice, mustard, and honey, stir until dissolved, and cook until it has slightly thickened, about 4 minutes. Add the oregano. Taste, and add the remaining pinch of salt, if desired.

4. Put 1 pork chop on each plate and top with the pan sauce. Serve immediately.

PER SERVING: Calories: 197; Total fat: 8g; Saturated fat: 2g; Sodium: 438g; Total carbohydrates: 6g; Sugar: 3g; Fiber: 1g; Protein: 26g; Calcium: 25mg

Pork and Veggie Skewers

DAIRY-FREE
GLUTEN-FEE
NUT-FREE
30-MINUTE

PREP TIME:
15 minutes

COOK TIME:
15 minutes

SERVES 4

These easy-to-make skewers bring to mind the shish kabobs of Turkish cuisine but with a touch of a beloved Spanish spice, smoked paprika. Grilling where I live is a year-round activity, but when you can't get outside to grill, you can easily make the skewers in the oven. Removing the mushroom stems makes it easier to slide the mushrooms onto the skewers without breaking them. Soaking wooden skewers is essential when using them in the oven or grill to ensure they do not catch fire during the cooking process.

8 (11¾-inch) metal or wooden skewers

1 pound pork tenderloin, cut into 1-inch cubes

8 ounces mushrooms, stems removed

1 large red bell pepper, stemmed, seeded, and cut into 1-inch pieces

1 small red onion, quartered and layers pulled apart

1 large yellow squash, cut into ½-inch rounds

¼ cup lemon juice

4 tablespoons olive oil

2 teaspoons smoked paprika

2 teaspoons garlic powder

2 teaspoons ground cumin

¾ teaspoon kosher salt

1. Preheat a charcoal or gas grill to medium heat. If using wooden skewers, soak them in water for 1 hour before using.

2. In a large bowl, combine the pork, mushrooms, bell pepper, onion, squash, lemon juice, oil, smoked paprika, garlic powder, cumin, and salt and, using your hands, toss the ingredients until evenly coated.

3. Thread the pork and veggies onto the skewers, alternating the pork and veggies on each skewer.

4. Grill the skewers for 3 to 4 minutes on each side. The pork should be cooked through and the veggies slightly charred on the edges, but not burnt.

5. Serve warm.

PER SERVING: Calories: 300; Total fat: 18g; Saturated fat: 3g; Sodium: 416g; Total carbohydrates: 12g; Sugar: 6g; Fiber: 3g; Protein: 25g; Calcium: 43mg

PREP TIME:
15 minutes

COOK TIME:
20 minutes

SERVES 6

Beef Meatballs with Sweet-and-Sour Pomegranate Glaze

I always use meatballs as an opportunity to add veggies such as mushrooms, herbs, spinach, and even zucchini. Not only do you get the nutrients from the vegetables, but you also extend the quantity of meat in order to make more meatballs, and to top it off, they are healthier because you consume less meat with each serving. Popular in Turkish, Lebanese, and Greek cuisine, pomegranate molasses is simply pomegranate juice that has boiled down to a sweet-and-sour syrup. The meatballs can be stored in the freezer, cooked or uncooked, for up to 4 months. Serve the meatballs over steamed white or brown basmati rice along with a simple green salad for a balanced full meal.

1 teaspoon olive oil
½ medium white onion,
   quartered
2 cups chopped fresh parsley
4 ounces mushrooms, halved
1 pound 90-percent lean
   ground beef
½ cup panko bread crumbs

1 egg
1 teaspoon ground cumin
¾ teaspoon coarse
   kosher salt
⅓ cup pomegranate
   molasses
1 teaspoon honey

1. Preheat the oven to 400°F. Line a sheet pan with a silicone baking mat or parchment paper and rub the oil on the mat.

2. Combine the onion, parsley, and mushrooms in a food processor and process until the mixture is smooth, scraping down the bowl when necessary.

3. Transfer the mixture to a large bowl. Add the beef, panko, egg, cumin, and salt and mix with your hands until well combined.

4. Form the mixture into 18 equal-size balls, each about the size of a large golf ball. Place them on the sheet pan and bake for 15 minutes.

5. In a small bowl, mix together the pomegranate molasses and honey to make the glaze.

6. Remove the pan from the oven and pour the glaze over the meatballs, rolling them around in the glaze to coat them.

7. Return the pan to the oven and bake for another 5 minutes.

8. Serve warm.

COOKING TIP: If you don't have a food processor, finely chop the mushrooms and parsley and grate the onion.

PER SERVING: Calories: 227; Total fat: 9g; Saturated fat: 3g; Sodium: 369g; Total carbohydrates: 19g; Sugar: 11g; Fiber: 1g; Protein: 18g; Calcium: 50mg

Mediterranean Steak Bowl with Bulgur, Hummus, and Feta

Steak, whole grains, and veggies in under 30 minutes? Oh yes you can! I love meals in a bowl that combine all these components, and I also like adding tasty toppings like hummus and feta. If you have some Tzatziki Sauce (page 170) on hand, you can use that in place of the hummus. Also, if you don't eat cheese, replace the feta with Kalamata olives; they have a similar salty tanginess.

½ cup bulgur
1 cup water
2 teaspoons olive oil
1 teaspoon dried oregano
¼ teaspoon coarse
   kosher salt
Pinch freshly ground
   black pepper
1¼ pounds flank steak

1⅓ cups halved cherry
   tomatoes
2 cups chopped English or
   Persian cucumber
½ cup Lemony Parsley
   Hummus (page 44) or
   store-bought hummus
⅓ cup crumbled feta cheese

1. Preheat a charcoal or gas grill to medium heat.

2. Combine the bulgur and water in a saucepan and bring to a boil. Cover the pot with a lid and turn off the heat. Let sit for 20 minutes.

3. Rub the oil, oregano, salt, and pepper all over the steak and transfer to a plate.

4. Place the flank steak on the hot grill and cook on each side until medium-rare and an instant-read thermometer reaches 130°F to 135°F, 5 to 6 minutes. The steak should have defined grill marks but not be burnt. Let it rest for 5 minutes.

5. Cut the steak against the grain into slices. Spoon the bulgur, tomatoes, and cucumbers into four bowls. Top with the steak, hummus, and feta cheese and serve.

COOKING TIP: If you don't have an outdoor grill, you can use a stovetop grill pan or broil the steak in the oven. To cook in the oven, broil each side for 4 to 6 minutes.

PER SERVING: Calories: 394; Total fat: 16g; Saturated fat: 6g; Sodium: 431g; Total carbohydrates: 23g; Sugar: 4g; Fiber: 6g; Protein: 40g; Calcium: 129mg

PREP TIME:
5 minutes

COOK TIME:
3 hours
10 minutes

SERVES 5

Balsamic and Red Wine Oven-Braised Brisket

The oven does most of the work here, not you. After a super quick prep, put the roast in the oven and forget about it. Flat-cut brisket is the most common cut of brisket found at the supermarket and my preferred thickness. The braising liquid should be reduced enough by the end of cooking, but if you want a thicker sauce, place the pot on the stove and cook for a few minutes, until the juices reduce a bit and are thick enough to coat the back of a spoon.

2 pounds flat-cut beef brisket, about 2 inches thick
¼ teaspoon coarse kosher salt, plus ⅛ teaspoon
Pinch freshly ground black pepper

1 tablespoon olive oil
2 yellow onions, thinly sliced
2 cups dry red wine
2 cups low-sodium beef broth
¼ cup balsamic vinegar

1. Preheat the oven to 325°F.

2. If your brisket has a thick fat cap on one side, trim it down with a knife, but don't remove all of it. Rub the meat with ¼ teaspoon of salt and the pepper.

3. Heat the oil in a wide, heavy-bottomed pot or Dutch oven over high heat until the oil is shimmering. Add the meat and sear until browned, 3 to 4 minutes on each side. Transfer the brisket to a plate. Discard all but 1 tablespoon of fat in the pan.

4. Add the onions to the pan and cook, stirring often, until they start to color, about 2 minutes.

5. Add the wine, broth, vinegar, and brisket, fat-side up, along with any juices, to the pan. Cover and bake for 3 hours, or until the beef is very tender, the onions are meltingly soft, and the juices have reduced.

6. Transfer the meat to a cutting board and let rest.

7. Taste the liquid in the pan and add the remaining ⅛ teaspoon of salt, if desired. If you prefer a thicker sauce, place the pan over high heat and cook until the liquid reduces to the desired consistency.

8. Cut the meat against the grain into slices and transfer to plates. Top with the pan juices and serve warm.

VARIATION TIP: You can add other veggies such as carrots, celery, parsnips, and potatoes. Add them 1 hour before the meat is done to ensure that they don't get mushy.

PER SERVING: Calories: 312; Total fat: 9g; Saturated fat: 2g; Sodium: 359g; Total carbohydrates: 11g; Sugar: 5g; Fiber: 1g; Protein: 28g; Calcium: 33mg

PREP TIME:
10 minutes

COOK TIME:
15 minutes

SERVES 4

Sheet Pan Steak with Roasted Mushrooms, Red Onion, and Pesto

I love a good sear on a steak, but I wanted this recipe to be simple and fast, so I put a sheet pan in the oven for a couple of minutes to get it hot before placing the steak on it, which helps brown the outside. I've also called for prepared pesto to drizzle over the top, but if you have an extra 15 minutes, I recommend serving it with Salsa Verde (page 167). The herbs and spicy kick of chiles really complement the steak. If you need a starch to round out your meal, a baked potato would taste great.

1 pound top sirloin steak
1 teaspoon olive oil, plus
   2 tablespoons
¾ teaspoon coarse kosher
   salt, divided
2 pinches freshly ground
   black pepper, divided
¾ teaspoon minced fresh
   rosemary, divided

½ teaspoon garlic powder
1 large red onion, cut into
   1-inch chunks
4 portobello mushroom caps,
   cut into thirds
¼ cup prepared pesto, at
   room temperature

1. Preheat the oven to broil on high. Line a sheet pan with aluminum foil.

2. Pat the steak dry with a paper towel and rub both sides with 1 teaspoon of oil, ½ teaspoon salt, a pinch of pepper, and ½ teaspoon of rosemary.

3. On the sheet pan, toss the onion and mushrooms with the remaining 2 tablespoons of oil, remaining ¼ teaspoon of rosemary, remaining ¼ teaspoon of salt, and a pinch of pepper. Arrange the veggies at both ends of the pan, leaving a spot in the middle for the steak. Broil for 2 minutes.

4. Remove the pan from the oven, carefully place the steaks in the center of the pan, and broil for 5 minutes.

5. Remove the pan from the oven and flip the veggies and steak. Return the pan to the oven and broil for another 4 to 5 minutes, or until the veggies are tender and the steak is golden and browned around the edges and an instant-read thermometer reads 130°F to 135°F for medium-rare.

6. Let the steak rest for at least 5 minutes.

7. Cut the steak against the grain into slices. Spoon the mushrooms, onions, and sliced steak on individual plates, drizzle with the pesto, and serve.

PER SERVING: Calories: 345; Total fat: 20g; Saturated fat: 4g; Sodium: 447g; Total carbohydrates: 11g; Sugar: 5g; Fiber: 3g; Protein: 31g; Calcium: 68mg

PREP TIME:
10 minutes

COOK TIME:
8 to 9 hours

SERVES 6

Slow Cooker Beef Short Rib Tagine

A tagine is a stew cooked in a pot with a cone-shaped lid and is popular in North Africa. You can get those same flavors using a slow cooker. And nothing is easier than combining a bunch of ingredients into a slow cooker right before going to bed and waking up to a fully cooked meal that you can serve for dinner later that night, right? This recipe is full of Moroccan flavors, including cinnamon, ginger, cumin, and paprika. The dates will melt into the other ingredients, giving the stew an unexpected touch of sweetness. You can store this dish in an airtight container in the freezer for up to 6 months.

2 pounds boneless short ribs
½ teaspoon coarse kosher salt, divided
⅛ teaspoon freshly ground black pepper
1 pound carrots, cut into 1-inch pieces
2 cups chopped yellow onion
1 (15-ounce) can low-sodium chickpeas, drained and rinsed

½ cup whole pitted dates
1 tablespoon paprika
2 teaspoons ground cumin
1 teaspoon ground ginger
½ teaspoon ground cinnamon
3 tablespoons tomato paste, dissolved in 1½ cups hot water

1. Season the short ribs with ¼ teaspoon of salt and the pepper.

2. Combine the ribs, carrots, onion, chickpeas, dates, paprika, cumin, ginger, cinnamon, and tomato paste mixture in a slow cooker, stir, and cook on low for 8 to 9 hours, or until the short ribs are very tender.

3. Taste, and season with the remaining ¼ teaspoon of salt, if desired.

PER SERVING: Calories: 348; Total fat: 13g; Saturated fat: 4g; Sodium: 255g; Total carbohydrates: 27g; Sugar: 14g; Fiber: 6g; Protein: 32g; Calcium: 71mg

Cocoa-Raspberry
Chia Pudding, *page 159*

Sweets, Sauces, and Staples

PREP TIME:
15 minutes

SERVES 4

Balsamic Strawberries with Whipped Vanilla Ricotta

Strawberries mixed with balsamic vinegar are a classic Italian sweet treat. The success of this dessert lies in the quality of the ricotta, so buy the best one you can find without additives such as gums and carrageenan. My favorite brand, which is sold at many large grocers, is BelGioioso. It's so smooth and creamy!

3 tablespoons balsamic vinegar
3 teaspoons honey, divided
1 pound fresh strawberries, hulled and quartered

1 cup whole-milk ricotta cheese
½ teaspoon pure vanilla extract

1. In a medium bowl, whisk together the vinegar and 2 teaspoons of honey. Add the strawberries, stir until coated, and let sit for 10 minutes.

2. While the strawberries are macerating, in a medium bowl, whisk together the ricotta, remaining 1 teaspoon of honey, and vanilla until smooth, about 30 seconds.

3. Place ¾ cup of strawberries into each of four small bowls or dessert glasses and pour any remaining liquid equally over the top. Spoon ¼ cup of the ricotta mixture over each serving and serve.

INGREDIENT TIP: If your ricotta is on the grainy side, try processing it in a food processor until it becomes smoother, about 1 minute. Because you'll probably have extra ricotta left in the container, use it the next day as a spread on toast. Top with sliced strawberries and a drizzle of honey for a delicious breakfast.

PER SERVING: Calories: 172; Total fat: 8g; Saturated fat: 5g; Sodium: 56g; Total carbohydrates: 17g; Sugar: 12g; Fiber: 2g; Protein: 8g; Calcium: 150mg

Cocoa-Raspberry Chia Pudding

DAIRY-FREE
5-INGREDIENT
GLUTEN-FREE
NO-COOK
VEGAN

PREP TIME:
5 minutes, plus
4 hours to set

SERVES 5

Chia pudding is literally one of the easiest sweet treats you can make. Combine a few ingredients, stir, refrigerate, and that's it! I have to admit, I also love eating this for breakfast. Chia seeds are nutritional powerhouses, rich in protein, omega-3s, fiber, and antioxidants. I always keep some on hand to make chia pudding or to add to yogurt parfaits and smoothies.

2¾ cups unsweetened soy milk

½ cup chia seeds

2 tablespoons pure maple syrup

⅓ cup unsweetened cocoa powder

1 cup frozen raspberries, thawed

Unsweetened coconut shavings, for topping (optional)

Fresh assorted berries, for topping (optional)

1. In a large bowl, whisk together the soy milk, chia, maple syrup, and cocoa powder. Let sit at room temperature for 15 minutes, whisking every 5 minutes to ensure a smooth pudding without lumps.

2. Cover the bowl and refrigerate, stirring the pudding every hour, until a thick pudding has formed, about 4 hours.

3. Spoon the thawed raspberries into bowls, followed by the pudding. Top with the coconut and fresh berries (if using) and serve.

INGREDIENT TIP: If you have any vanilla extract on hand, pour in ½ teaspoon. The flavor of the vanilla is a nice complement to the cocoa.

PER SERVING: Calories: 193; Total fat: 10g; Saturated fat: 1g; Sodium: 52g; Total carbohydrates: 23g; Sugar: 7g; Fiber: 11g; Protein: 8g; Calcium: 317mg

PREP TIME:
10 minutes,
plus 2 hours
15 minutes
to freeze

COOK TIME:
2 minutes

SERVES 8

Frozen Peanut Butter and Jelly Chocolate-Covered Bananas

Two of my favorite things to eat as a kid were peanut butter and jelly sandwiches and chocolate-covered frozen bananas. I've combined both into a fun, small-bite sweet treat, inspired by the fruit-forward desserts around the Mediterranean (but with an American twist). Dark chocolate is heart-healthy due to antioxidants called flavonoids, an added health-forward bonus. I love raspberry preserves for this dessert, but you can use whatever flavor you like. If your olive oil is very strong tasting, use a neutral oil such as canola.

2 ripe 8-inch bananas, cut into 32 (¼-inch-thick) slices

4 teaspoons natural-style smooth peanut butter

4 teaspoons raspberry preserves, preferably all-fruit, no-sugar-added

¾ cup dark chocolate chips, preferably 60 percent cacao or higher

1 teaspoon olive oil

1. Line a large dinner plate with parchment paper. Place half of the banana slices on the plate. Top each slice with ¼ teaspoon of peanut butter, ¼ teaspoon of raspberry preserves, and another banana slice. It's fine if the preserves and peanut butter ooze over the sides. Repeat until you have 16 "sandwiches."

2. Place the banana sandwiches in the freezer for at least 2 hours, or until fully firm.

3. Just before you're ready to take the bananas out of the freezer, place the chocolate chips and oil in a microwave-safe bowl and microwave on high for 30 seconds. Stir and continue microwaving in 20-second increments, stirring after each time, until the chocolate is melted. It should only take a few rounds to fully melt the chips.

4. Remove the bananas from the freezer, dip half of the sandwich into the chocolate, and return to the plate. Repeat with the other banana sandwiches. Freeze for 15 minutes to harden the chocolate.

5. Place the banana sandwiches in an airtight container and store in the freezer until ready to eat, or up to 1 month.

INGREDIENT TIP: Be sure to check the ingredient list on the chocolate chip label if you are dairy-free because some brands may include dairy-based ingredients.

PER SERVING: Calories: 164; Total fat: 9g; Saturated fat: 4g; Sodium: 15g; Total carbohydrates: 20g; Sugar: 13g; Fiber: 3g; Protein: 2g; Calcium: 15mg

PREP TIME:
15 minutes

COOK TIME:
30 minutes

SERVES 8

Lemon, Cornmeal, and Yogurt Cake

Lucky for all of us, the Mediterranean diet isn't sugar-free. Sweets are eaten sparingly, but it's perfectly fine to indulge your sweet tooth on occasion. Because my household includes only two people, an entire cake is just too much. That's why I love this cake. Leftovers can be frozen until you have another craving for sweets.

Nonstick cooking spray or olive oil, for greasing
½ cup cornmeal
1 cup all-purpose flour
1½ teaspoons baking powder
⅛ teaspoon kosher salt
3 large eggs

½ cup low-fat (2 percent) plain Greek yogurt
¼ cup olive oil
1 cup granulated sugar, divided
Zest and juice of 2 lemons

1. Preheat the oven to 350°F. Coat a 9-inch round cake pan with cooking spray or rub it all over with a thin layer of oil.

2. In a large bowl, whisk together the cornmeal, flour, baking powder, and salt until just combined.

3. In a separate bowl, whisk together the eggs, yogurt, oil, ¾ cup of sugar, lemon zest, and 2 tablespoons of lemon juice, until smooth.

4. Pour the wet ingredients into the dry ingredients and stir just until blended. Do not overmix.

5. Pour the batter into the prepared cake pan and bake for 25 to 30 minutes, or until the edges are golden and a paring knife comes out clean when inserted.

6. Combine the remaining ¼ cup of sugar and 2 tablespoons of lemon juice in a saucepan and heat on low until the sugar dissolves, about 1 minute.

7. When the pan is cool enough to handle, run a knife around the edge of the cake, invert the pan, and tap the bottom to remove the cake onto a large plate. Poke about 10 holes into the top of the cake and slowly pour the lemon glaze over the cake.

8. Let cool completely before cutting into slices or freezing.

STORAGE TIP: To freeze the whole cake for up to 3 months, wrap the cooled cake in two layers of plastic wrap and a layer of aluminum foil and place in the freezer. When ready to eat, defrost the cake at room temperature for about 3 hours before cutting into slices.

PER SERVING: Calories: 353; Total fat: 10g; Saturated fat: 2g; Sodium: 67g; Total carbohydrates: 63g; Sugar: 44g; Fiber: 1g; Protein: 6g; Calcium: 111mg

PREP TIME:
5 minutes

COOK TIME:
45 minutes

SERVES 4

White Wine–Poached Pears with Cinnamon and Pistachios

Poached pears are the epitome of a classic fruit dessert—simple, elegant, and sweet. If you're in the mood for a dessert that's a bit more decadent, top the poached pears with a small scoop of vanilla ice cream, crème fraîche, mascarpone, or plain Greek yogurt.

2 cups Riesling wine

1 cup water

⅓ cup honey

2 cinnamon sticks

4 firm but ripe Bosc pears

¼ cup shelled pistachios, coarsely chopped

1. In a 3- or 4-quart saucepan, combine the wine, water, honey, and cinnamon sticks and stir until the honey is dissolved. Bring to a vigorous simmer over medium-high heat.

2. While the liquid is heating, peel the pears, cut them in half vertically, and core them with a melon baller or spoon.

3. Add the pears to the pot, lower the heat to medium-low, and simmer until the pears are tender, but not mushy, 25 to 30 minutes.

4. Transfer the pears to a plate and set aside.

5. Increase the heat to high and cook until the liquid reduces to about ½ cup and it's syrupy and darker in color, 12 to 15 minutes.

6. Place 2 pear halves on each plate, spoon about 1 tablespoon of the syrup over the pears, and sprinkle the pistachios over the top. Serve immediately.

VARIATION TIP: Serving the pears chilled is also a delicious option. After cooking, let the pears and syrup cool completely. Place the pears and syrup in an airtight container and refrigerate until chilled.

PER SERVING: Calories: 344; Total fat: 4g; Saturated fat: 1g; Sodium: 5g; Total carbohydrates: 57g; Sugar: 42g; Fiber: 6g; Protein: 2g; Calcium: 29mg

Apple Vinaigrette

DAIRY-FREE
15-MINUTE
5-INGREDIENT
GLUTEN-FREE
NO-COOK
NUT-FREE
VEGAN

Fruit juice of all kinds make tasty bases for homemade salad dressing. You could use pomegranate, orange, or even pineapple juice in a vinaigrette. Whenever you use fruit juice in a salad dressing, make sure that it is 100 percent juice without any added sugar. When using this vinaigrette on your salad, add some sliced green apple to complement the apple juice in the dressing.

PREP TIME:
5 minutes

MAKES ½ CUP

1 tablespoon apple
  cider vinegar
⅓ cup apple juice
2 tablespoons minced shallot

½ teaspoon honey
⅛ teaspoon coarse kosher salt
3 tablespoons olive oil

1. In a small bowl, whisk together the vinegar, apple juice, shallot, honey, and salt.

2. Add the oil in a thin stream, whisking constantly, until the mixture emulsifies into a thick dressing.

STORAGE TIP: You can store homemade salad dressing in an airtight container in the refrigerator for up to 2 weeks.

PER SERVING (2 TABLESPOONS): Calories: 106; Total fat: 11g; Saturated fat: 2g; Sodium: 62g; Total carbohydrates: 4g; Sugar: 3g; Fiber: 0g; Protein: 0g; Calcium: 4mg

DAIRY-FREE
15-MINUTE
5-INGREDIENT
GLUTEN-FREE
NO-COOK
NUT-FREE
VEGAN

PREP TIME:
5 minutes

MAKES ½ CUP

Lemon-Dijon Vinaigrette

Homemade salad dressing is very easy to make and can really elevate any salad into something special. Inspired by the classic vinaigrettes of France, this recipe is the "house" dressing in my home and is requested by my husband several times a week. In addition to dressing salads, you can drizzle it over chicken, fish, and veggies or use it as a marinade.

¼ **cup lemon juice**
2 **teaspoons Dijon mustard**

⅛ **teaspoon coarse**
   kosher salt
¼ **cup olive oil**

1. In a small bowl, whisk together the lemon juice, mustard, and salt.

2. Add the oil in a thin stream, whisking constantly, until the mixture emulsifies into a thick dressing.

PER SERVING (2 TABLESPOONS): Calories: 126; Total fat: 14g; Saturated fat: 2g; Sodium: 125g; Total carbohydrates: 1g; Sugar: 0g; Fiber: 0g; Protein: 0g; Calcium: 1mg

Salsa Verde (Green Herb Sauce)

DAIRY-FREE
15-MINUTE
GLUTEN-FREE
NO-COOK
NUT-FREE

PREP TIME:
15 minutes

MAKES 1 CUP

When you hear the words *salsa verde*, you may automatically think of a Mexican-style green salsa made from chiles and tomatillos. However, in the Mediterranean—specifically Italy—salsa verde refers to a sauce made with herbs, capers, and anchovies. If you are reluctant to use anchovies, give this a chance. The anchovies are there for flavor without being fishy at all. In fact, you probably won't even know that they're in there. This flavor-packed sauce reminds me of a cross between a chimichurri and a basil pesto, and I think it's perfect for drizzling over steak, chicken, fish, veggies, or baked tofu.

2 cups packed fresh basil

2 cups packed fresh parsley

2 large garlic cloves

¼ teaspoon red chili flakes

1 tablespoon capers, drained and rinsed

3 anchovy fillets

¼ teaspoon coarse kosher salt

2 tablespoons lemon juice

⅓ cup olive oil

¼ cup water, plus 1 or 2 tablespoons, if needed

1. Combine the basil, parsley, garlic, chili flakes, capers, anchovies, salt, lemon juice, oil, and ½ cup of water in a blender and blend until smooth, scraping the sides down when necessary.

2. If the sauce isn't coming together, add more water, 1 tablespoon at a time, until the ingredients in the blender thin out and start blending more easily.

COOKING TIP: You can also make this sauce in a food processor.

PER SERVING (2 TABLESPOONS): Calories: 89; Total fat: 10g; Saturated fat: 1g; Sodium: 148g; Total carbohydrates: 1g; Sugar: 0g; Fiber: 0g; Protein: 1g; Calcium: 27mg

PREP TIME:
5 minutes

MAKES 1 CUP

Smoked Paprika Aioli

Known as aioli in France and alioli in Spain, this creamy sauce is basically a garlic mayonnaise. For this super-easy version, I've enhanced prepared mayonnaise and lightened it up with a little Greek yogurt. I love that it's not necessary to chop a single ingredient. This sauce would pair very well with Pan-Seared Halibut (page 124) or any roasted or grilled meat or veggie. A dollop on top of the Veggie Paella (page 100) would taste great, too.

⅔ cup low-fat (2 percent)
   plain Greek yogurt
⅓ cup mayonnaise
1 teaspoon garlic powder
1½ teaspoons
   smoked paprika

⅛ teaspoon cayenne pepper
1 teaspoon olive oil
¼ teaspoon coarse
   kosher salt

1. In a medium bowl, mix together the yogurt, mayonnaise, garlic powder, smoked paprika, cayenne, oil, and salt until well combined.

2. Add additional cayenne if you like it spicy.

PER SERVING (2 TABLESPOONS): Calories: 83; Total fat: 8g; Saturated fat: 1g; Sodium: 125g; Total carbohydrates: 1g; Sugar: 1g; Fiber: 0g; Protein: 2g; Calcium: 23mg

Garlic Tahini Sauce

When I first made this tahini sauce, it was so good that I kept eating it on its own! It really is that tasty and super quick to make. Tahini consists of sesame seeds that are ground into a paste, and it's a very popular ingredient in countries all over the eastern Mediterranean. Drizzle it over meat, veggies, and grain bowls.

DAIRY-FREE
15-MINUTE
5-INGREDIENT
GLUTEN-FREE
NO-COOK
NUT-FREE
VEGAN

PREP TIME:
5 minutes

MAKES 1 CUP

½ cup unsalted tahini
½ cup cold water
½ teaspoon garlic powder
⅛ teaspoon ground cumin

Pinch cayenne pepper
2 tablespoons lemon juice
¼ teaspoon coarse kosher salt

1. In a medium bowl, whisk together tahini and the water, 2 tablespoons at a time, until you have a pale, creamy, and pourable sauce.

2. Add the garlic powder, cumin, pepper, lemon juice, and salt and whisk until combined.

INGREDIENT TIP: Tahini can vary in thickness from brand to brand. If your sauce seems too thick for your taste, whisk in more water, 1 tablespoon at a time.

PER SERVING (2 TABLESPOONS): Calories: 112; Total fat: 10g; Saturated fat: 2g; Sodium: 69g; Total carbohydrates: 2g; Sugar: 0g; Fiber: 2g; Protein: 4g; Calcium: 1.5mg

Tzatziki Sauce

Tzatziki is a traditional Greek yogurt sauce that can be used as a dip with crackers and veggies or as a sauce for grilled meats, or you can just eat it with a spoon! To save time, I've removed a step that involves salting and straining the chopped cucumbers to remove excess water. With the chopped cucumber, I don't feel that salting and straining it makes a huge difference in the final product. If you make this sauce in advance and you see some liquid collecting in the bowl, just stir it up, and it will be as good as new.

5 ounces English or Persian
  cucumber, cut into
  ¼-inch pieces
1 (17.6-ounce) container
  low-fat (2 percent) plain
  Greek yogurt
1 tablespoon olive oil
2 teaspoons lemon juice

½ teaspoon chopped garlic
½ teaspoon coarse
  kosher salt
⅛ teaspoon freshly ground
  black pepper
2 tablespoons chopped
  fresh dill

1. In a medium bowl, mix together the cucumber, yogurt, oil, lemon juice, garlic, salt, pepper, and dill until combined.

2. Taste, and add more lemon juice, if desired.

3. Serve cold or at room temperature.

VARIATION TIP: Feel free to add some freshly chopped mint if you have it to give it an added bright flavor.

PER SERVING (½ CUP): Calories: 100; Total fat: 5g; Saturated fat: 0g; Sodium: 226g; Total carbohydrates: 4g; Sugar: 4g; Fiber: 0g; Protein: 10g; Calcium: 116mg

Measurement Conversions

Volume Equivalents	U.S. Standard	U.S. Standard (ounces)	Metric (approximate)
Liquid	2 tablespoons	1 fl. oz.	30 mL
	¼ cup	2 fl. oz.	60 mL
	½ cup	4 fl. oz.	120 mL
	1 cup	8 fl. oz.	240 mL
	1½ cups	12 fl. oz.	355 mL
	2 cups or 1 pint	16 fl. oz.	475 mL
	4 cups or 1 quart	32 fl. oz.	1 L
	1 gallon	128 fl. oz.	4 L
Dry	⅛ teaspoon	—	0.5 mL
	¼ teaspoon	—	1 mL
	½ teaspoon	—	2 mL
	¾ teaspoon	—	4 mL
	1 teaspoon	—	5 mL
	1 tablespoon	—	15 mL
	¼ cup	—	59 mL
	⅓ cup	—	79 mL
	½ cup	—	118 mL
	⅔ cup	—	156 mL
	¾ cup	—	177 mL
	1 cup	—	235 mL
	2 cups or 1 pint	—	475 mL
	3 cups	—	700 mL
	4 cups or 1 quart	—	1 L
	½ gallon	—	2 L
	1 gallon	—	4 L

Oven Temperatures

Fahrenheit	Celsius (approximate)
250°F	120°C
300°F	150°C
325°F	165°C
350°F	180°C
375°F	190°C
400°F	200°C
425°F	220°C
450°F	230°C

Weight Equivalents

U.S. Standard	Metric (approximate)
½ ounce	15 g
1 ounce	30 g
2 ounces	60 g
4 ounces	115 g
8 ounces	225 g
12 ounces	340 g
16 ounces or 1 pound	455 g

References

Cabral, Danylo F., Jordyn Rice, Timothy P. Morris, Tajana Rundek, Alvaro Pascual-Leone, and Joyce Gomes-Osman. "Exercise for Brain Health: An Investigation into the Underlying Mechanisms Guided by Dose." *Neurotherapeutics* 16, no. 3 (2019): 580–99.

Centers for Disease Control and Prevention. "How Much Physical Activity Do Adults Need?" Last reviewed October 7, 2020. CDC.gov/physicalactivity /basics/adults/index.htm.

Davis, Courtney, Janet Bryan, Jonathan Hodgson, and Karen Murphy. "Definition of the Mediterranean Diet: A Literature Review." *Nutrients* 7, no. 11 (November 2015): 9139–53.

Franquesa, Marcella, Georgina Pujol-Busquets, Elena García-Fernández, Laura Rico, Laia Shamirian-Pulido, Alicia Aguilar-Martínez, Francesc Xavier Medina, et al. "Mediterranean Diet and Cardiodiabesity: A Systematic Review through Evidence-Based Answers to Key Clinical Questions." *Nutrients* 11, no. 3 (2019): 655.

Godos, Justyna, Raffaele Ferri, Filippo Caraci, Filomena Irene Ilaria Cosentino, Sabrina Castellano, Fabio Galvano, and Giuseppe Grosso. "Adherence to the Mediterranean Diet Is Associated with Better Sleep Quality in Italian Adults." *Nutrients* 11, no. 5 (2019): 976.

Logsdon, Aric F., Michelle A. Erickson, Elizabeth M. Rhea, Therese S. Salmeh, and William A. Banks. "Gut Reactions: How the Blood-Brain Barrier Connects the Microbiome and the Brain." *Experimental Biology and Medicine* 243, no. 2 (2019): 159–65.

Mentella, Maria Chiara, Franco Scaldaferri, Caterina Ricci, Antonio Gasbarrini, and Giacinto Abele Donato Miggiano. "Cancer and Mediterranean Diet: A Review." *Nutrients* 11, no. 9 (2019): 2059.

Sánchez-Villegas, Almudena, Jacqueline Álvarez-Pérez, Estefanía Toledo, Jordi Salas-Salvadó, Carolina Ortega-Azorín, Maria Dolores Zomeño, Jesús

Vioque, et al. "Seafood Consumption, Omega-3 Fatty Acids Intake, and Life-Time Prevalence of Depression in the PREDIMED-Plus Trial." *Nutrients* 10, no. 12 (2018): 2000.

Sánchez-Villegas, Almudena, Miguel Ruíz-Canela, Alfredo Gea, Francisco Lahortiga, and Miguel A. Martínez-González. "The Association between the Mediterranean Lifestyle and Depression." *Clinical Psychological Science* 4, no. 6 (2016): 1085–93.

Schwingshackl, Lukas, Jakub Morze, and Georg Hoffman. "Mediterranean Diet and Health Status: Active Ingredients and Pharmacological Mechanisms." *British Journal of Pharmacology* 177, no. 6 (2020): 1241–57.

Tian, Danyang, and Jinqi Meng. "Exercise for Prevention and Relief of Cardiovascular Disease: Prognoses, Mechanisms, and Approaches." *Oxidative Medicine and Cellular Longevity* (2019): 3756750.

Tosti, Valeria, Beatrice Bertozzi, and Luigi Fontana. "Health Benefits of the Mediterranean Diet: Metabolic and Molecular Mechanisms." *The Journals of Gerontology* 73, no. 3 (2018): 318–26.

Umberson, Debra, and Jennifer Karas Montez. "Social Relationships and Health: A Flashpoint for Health Policy." *Journal of Health and Social Behavior* 51, no. S1 (2010): S54–S66.

Recipe Label Index

30-MINUTE

Index

Acknowledgments

Thank you to my husband for putting up with a very messy kitchen over the course of writing this book and for encouraging me to take opportunities that challenge me. I have much gratitude for my family and loved ones for always supporting my career endeavors. Thank you to Chef Rachel Paghunasan for introducing me to the wonders of tofu ricotta and for allowing me to adapt her recipe for my dish. Last but not least, thank you to Vanessa Putt for giving me this opportunity as well as editors Adrian Potts and Cecily McAndrews for their input and guidance.

About the Author

LINDSEY PINE, RD, MS, is the owner of TastyBalance Nutrition, specializing in recipe development and nutrition communications that support a heart-healthy lifestyle. In addition to writing her own blog, she has contributed to numerous publications, including *Campus Dining Today*, *Today's Dietitian*, *Self*, and *Reader's Digest*.

Lindsey is also the dining dietitian for USC Hospitality on the campus of the University of Southern California. Her education includes a culinary degree from Seattle Central Community College, a bachelor's degree in hospitality and tourism management from San Diego State University, and a master's degree in nutritional science from Cal State LA.

She and her husband currently reside in her hometown of Los Angeles.

CPSIA information can be obtained
at www.ICGtesting.com
Printed in the USA
JSHW010912210122
22151JS00001B/1